Dean McElwee

ISBN: 978-1-3999-5766-3

ECOMMERCE FOR CEOS

WHAT EVERY CEO AND C-SUITE LEADER SHOULD KNOW ABOUT ECOMMERCE

DEAN MCELWEE

ACKNOWLEDGEMENTS

I would like to extend my heartfelt thanks to several industry colleagues who have been instrumental in this finished manuscript. Todd Hassenfelt from Colgate Palmolive, Kiri Masters from Acadia, Joseph Harper from Diageo, Niall O'Gorman from Channelsight and Lauren Livak from The Digital Shelf Institute. Their peer review immeasurably improved the overall book itself but challenged the messages that this book conveys improving it with each iteration.

The inspiration for this book came from Kiri Masters an accomplished author in her own right with Instacart for CMOs, Amazon for CMOs and The Amazon Expansion Plan. Her commitment to inspiring and educating industry colleagues laid the foundation for this work.

The production of a book does not happen without countless hours of correction. Special thanks to Lauren Livak for the cover design and endless editing!

Lastly the support of my family and most importantly my wife has meant the world to me as I have finalized this work. I am incredibly humbled by the support that I have received.

Contents

INTRODUCTION

Chapter 1 / Decoding what eCommerce is

Chapter 2 / The Case for eCommerce

Chapter 3 / Why is eCommerce different and how should you approach marketing in the digital age

Chapter 4 / The eCommerce Amplification Effect

Chapter 5 / A Primer on eCommerce Go To Market Strategy

CHAPTER 6 / Omnichannel

CHAPTER 7 / Online Marketplaces

CHAPTER 8 / Direct to Consumer

CHAPTER 9 / Business to Business

CHAPTER 10 / Retail Media

CHAPTER 11 / Measuring your ecommerce performance

CHAPTER 12 / Building a winning ecommerce organization

CHAPTER 13 / What's next for ecommerce

Glossary of eCommerce Terms

Bibliography

INTRODUCTION

In the last two weeks of March 2020, search interest on Google for the term 'online shopping' peaked worldwide[1]. The search interest began peaking as the world had to swiftly adjust to an altered shopping environment brought on by the advent of a global pandemic. Shoppers who use this term in the context of shopping were adjusting.

Initially in boardrooms across the world, this was seen as a temporary situation, however, in due course, it would prove not to be. In the following month, many businesses grappled as they came to terms, most of them remotely with a business environment that would change dramatically, changing the way they did business and the way their partners operated. From the 19th of April 2020, the business community had adjusted and searches on Google started increasing for two key terms: 'eCommerce' and its sibling 'E-Commerce' which are the commonly used terms within the business community to describe what is online shopping to consumers[2]. These terms remained at elevated levels of search on Google for the next four months as many came to grips with what would be a new reality for businesses. This indicates that companies and their business leaders were finally coming to terms with anew and altered reality. My hypothesis and personal experience was that most companies and executives found themselves caught unawares with the speed and quantum of the change.

Many businesses had invested in eCommerce, however, the sheer scale of what was to follow caught many business leaders unaware. Suddenly the revenue from eCommerce in many Consumer-Packaged Goods businesses and retailers went from contributing mid-single digits to swiftly contributing greater than 10 % and much more in many cases.

Many business leaders who had delegated the operation of their eCommerce business to a specialized team found themselves needing to upskill themselves and their teams to take advantage of the disproportionate growth in their eCommerce business relative to other channels of business.

Why I wrote this book

The tremendous and sustained growth in eCommerce in the years 2020-2021 accelerated eCommerce growth by at least five years and has meant that many business leaders have needed to review their business models, their team operations, and indeed their business go-to-market strategies at unprecedented levels. This has meant many may have made less informed choices than in other situations with mixed results.

In my experience, the Digital IQ, or the ability to harness and profit from technology of business leaders is often, but not always, inversely proportional to their seniority in organizations. This is not intended as a negative observation. It is reflective of the speed with which digital and eCommerce have accelerated and how we are all in essence trying to keep up with technology that didn't exist in the years when we entered the workforce. There is of course a generational construct to this. Senior business leaders have experienced tremendous change in their careers, whilst more junior and younger team members have grown up with technology at their fingertips. This means that younger generations may be more digitally literate than those who are deciding on a strategy. This disparity means that the leaders who are responsible for setting the strategic direction of the company may have less context as to how eCommerce can transform businesses. This means that organizations in many cases are unable to fully benefit from the growth in eCommerce and often may leave opportunities untapped.

This book, therefore, is for CEOs and C-Suite leaders who need to 'translate' what exists in the traditional environments they are comfortable with to this increasingly important environment of eCommerce. Many CEOs' success is grounded in knowledge of brick-and-mortar environments. For many there is no similar foundation in eCommerce. This book helps to connect the brick and mortar and digital worlds, creating a solid foundation for both.

Equally, many eCommerce leaders have spent much of their careers in this space. This book is also for them. eCommerce is important, but so is understanding omnichannel retail. There may well be eCommerce leaders who have spent their time with Digitally Native brands as it will assist them in understanding the brick-and-mortar retail environments which they may not be familiar with. The ability to connect both omni-channel and digital environments with equal dexterity will be a necessity for the C-Suite of the future. These leaders will benefit from the ability to more effectively and succinctly translate concepts from the eCommerce world into the omnichannel world to aid executive buy-in.

Lastly, this book is meant as a guide for business leaders who are either early in their journey or are faced with a transition in their career where it is now necessary to lead teams in charge of eCommerce growth. It is meant to assist you in translating what eCommerce is and how to capture as much of the growth as there is to have in eCommerce.

Not understanding what eCommerce is all about is no longer an option for CEOs, the C-Suite, and senior leaders. eCommerce is now pervasive as a way of doing business, as a business model, and as a channel of doing business and it is of the utmost importance that all business leaders at all levels learn how to leverage eCommerce in their business.

Why listen to me?

I have worked across both emerging and developed markets for Fortune 500 companies: The Stanley Black & Decker Company, The Kellogg Company, The Coca-Cola Company, Mastercard, and FMCG giant Nestle in both local, European, and global roles. My career has spanned consumer packaged goods that are perishable and those that aren't as well as consulting. I've been at the coalface of these companies as they have navigated and come to terms with an omnichannel world but also as they have refined approaches to business giants like Amazon. I've worked on both offline and online commercial strategies, so I have a detailed understanding of what makes both work. During my career, I've been incredibly fortunate to work with and on omnichannel and eCommerce retailers and studiously watched retailers and consumer packaged goods companies continuously evolve to meet the needs of demanding shoppers and consumers.

I'm interested in data and people in equal measure. I see what data points are most relevant to an issue and will use this ability to understand "What's going on?".

I'm interested in "why?" it explains the way in which individuals behave, and what drives them. It's this curiosity and desire to get to the root cause that helps me to decode and explain how concepts work.

At heart, I'm an architect and engineer that desires to create and build immaculate solutions that will stand the test of time. I've worked across both national, regional, and global roles. I'm equally at home with Omnichannel and eCommerce and understand what makes each of them work. I study people, what drives them, and how I can help them achieve what they and the business need. I know that Digital has the ability to transform how businesses operate, not just from an eCommerce perspective but across the entire business.

Chapter 1 / Decoding what eCommerce is

೦೪೮೦

So, what is eCommerce? The term E-Commerce was first used by Dr. Robert Jacobson, Principal Consultant to the California State Assembly's Utilities & Commerce Committee, in the title and text of California's Electronic Commerce Act enacted in 1984[1]. In this act, E-Commerce was clearly described as "electronic commercial services" which are defined as "electronic shopping systems" designed "to conduct the purchase of goods and services via a telecommunications network." E-Commerce, eCommerce, or electronic commerce is therefore the activity of electronically buying or selling of products on online services or over the web.

It is generally accepted that the earliest version of electronic shopping occurred in 1979 when Michael Aldrich connected a TV to a computer via a telephone line, creating the foundation for what would become online shopping[2]. The world's first eCommerce company followed shortly thereafter in 1982. This was the Boston Computer Exchange and the company dominated electronic trading in used computers in the 1980s[3]. The exchange was a marketplace and was the foundation for what would become automated trading. However, it was with the creation of the web in 1990[4] by Tim Berners-Lee that eCommerce, as we know it today, really began to take shape.

I am known by many names

Many practitioners and industry professionals have a favorite term either eCommerce or E-Commerce. Many discussions have taken place over the years as to which one is correct. Indeed, several more debates have been dedicated to whether eCommerce should just be referred to as commerce. Neither to my knowledge is incorrect, they are merely variations to describe the same thing.

Google's Trends tool analyzes the popularity of top search terms in Google search. Google Trends then uses this to graph the volume of searches. The first usage statistics from Google Trends indicate that E-Commerce was the globally dominant term from Google Trends' inception in January 2004 till mid-2009[5], but subsequently, eCommerce has been the globally preferred term. Interestingly the term E-Commerce is still the preferred term in Central Africa, China, Poland, and Belgium. As eCommerce is the globally preferred term on Google Trends, this will be used going forward in this book. Now that we have a foundational understanding of what eCommerce is, let's proceed with understanding the different iterations that eCommerce can take.

High-Level Business Models

There are several business models used to describe eCommerce. These describe the relationships between the two parties involved. These are overarching business models and within these are more detailed versions of the business models which will be explained in greater detail. Let's explore these in more detail:

Business to Consumer(B2C) describes electronic commerce where there are intermediaries involved such as wholesalers, retailers, or online marketplaces. Examples of B2C eCommerce platforms are Amazon, Wayfair, eBay, Allegro, JD.com, Walmart, LeClerc, Loblaws, Suning, and Tesco. The intermediary handles aspects such as inventory management, order fulfillment, and customer service. This is the most well-known form of eCommerce. Goods and services will be purchased using an online web portal or via a mobile application(app) on the user's mobile device. There is normally a clear target market in this business model and a short sales cycle in comparison to other forms of commerce.

Business to Business(B2B) describes electronic commerce between two businesses or representatives of two businesses. Examples of this model are Diageo One, the global liquor giant's business to business platform, and AB Inbev's Bees platform, the beer market leader that provides a substantial ordering platform in multiple countries for its customers. It is often used as a means to improve the efficiency and effectiveness of doing business between the two businesses. Instead of purchasing goods and services by interacting with representatives in a manual fashion such as through a sales rep, by telephone, fax, or email, orders are received via electronic means.

Consumer to Consumer or Peer to Peer(C2C) is a business model where commerce occurs between two private consumers without a business participating on either end of the transaction. These will be facilitated by a third party. Examples of these are Facebook Marketplace, Vinted, Depop and Craigslist.

Direct to Consumer (D2C or DTC) describes electronic commerce where a business chooses to eliminate intermediaries and establish a direct connection between the brand and the consumer. Examples of this business model are Gymshark, an athletic wear brand and Allbirds who are known for their footwear. An example of this could also be Nike and Adidas who both have successful DTC sites in addition to their existing routes to market. These websites are built and owned by the company or brand.

Chapter 2 / The Case for eCommerce

CR&O

eCommerce has been part of the fabric of business for the last three decades. It seems therefore that the opportunity and the business need for it should be well established. In relative terms however it is immature, retailing in some shape or form has been around for a long time. However, as we've discussed above, eCommerce comes in many different forms and therefore it is worth looking in more detail to understand some of the stimuli for its growth.

Internet users become Digital Buyers

Many consumers use the Internet for research, to consume news, or for entertainment purposes. As internet access continues to increase globally, so does the possibility that these users will go on to become digital buyers[1,2].

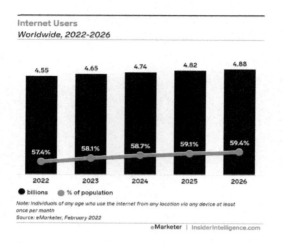

Above: Internet Users

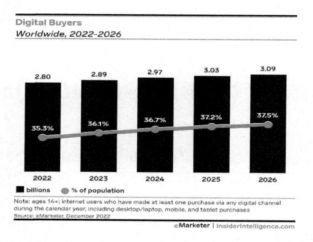

Above: Digital Buyers

The reality is that internet penetration is still below 60% but increasing. Internet connectivity is a prerequisite for eCommerce so as this continues to increase it follows that so should the proportion of people that go on to be digital buyers. In 2022 the gap between those who are internet users, but not digital shoppers were 1.75 billion people. This alone shows the tremendous potential for eCommerce growth.

The transformation from internet usage to digital shopping is not an easy one for consumers to make. There are several challenges that consumers need to overcome to become digital shoppers. These are:

- **Trust** - Many consumers are skeptical about providing their card (and personal details) over the Internet. Equally, trust that delivery will in fact take place for the items ordered is another challenge to overcome.
- **Affinity with technology** - Many consumers have not grown up with technology and therefore adoption of digital shopping is possibly harder, this is especially true of older demographics.
- **Infrastructure** - There are several prerequisites to digital shopping development: internet access with reasonable speeds, a bank account, fantastic postal or courier delivery, and secure internet servers.
- **Smartphone penetration** - As smartphone penetration increases, eCommerce follows as most online purchases are made on smartphones (We will cover more on the rise of mobile in the next chapter).

Clearly from a business-to-consumer perspective, the opportunity and case for eCommerce exists. However, an equally large opportunity is the one that exists with business-to-business eCommerce. US B2B eCommerce site sales are forecast to exceed 2.4 trillion dollars by 2026, as seen on the following page.

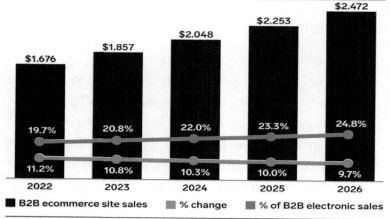

US B2B Ecommerce Site Sales, 2022-2026
trillions, % change, and % of B2B electronic sales

	2022	2023	2024	2025	2026
B2B ecommerce site sales	$1.676	$1.857	$2.048	$2.253	$2.472
% change	19.7%	20.8%	22.0%	23.3%	24.8%
% of B2B electronic sales	11.2%	10.8%	10.3%	10.0%	9.7%

■ B2B ecommerce site sales   ■ % change   ■ % of B2B electronic sales

Note: B2B product sales are the sale of physical products from one business to another, including sales from manufacturers, wholesalers, distributors, and retailers to other businesses; B2B electronic sales are the electronic sale of physical products from one business to another that occurs over the internet via an electronic data interchange (EDI), web-based ecommerce sites, or other online systems; B2B ecommerce sales are the sale of physical products from one business to another that occurs over the internet via an ecommerce site, including sales directly from a supplier website or indirectly through third-party online stores like marketplaces; includes online orders placed via any device, regardless of the method of payment or fulfillment
Source: eMarketer, Aug 2022

277982   eMarketer | InsiderIntelligence.com

Above: US B2B eCommerce Site Sales

B2B is less heralded than its consumer-facing peer. But its sheer size far outstrips the retail market. Several factors are driving the adoption of B2B within the workplace. These are:

- **Efficiency** - Many organizations that rely on phone, fax, or email for order placement and order inquiry are turning to eCommerce to improve efficiency.
- **Marketplaces** - The rise of marketplaces is forcing manufacturers to provide their own alternatives to the likes of Amazon.
- **Digitally native workforce** - A digitally native workforce is increasingly looking for vendors that provide ease of doing business and are permanently available.

- **Self-Service portals** - Business buyers are often looking to self-serve and becoming more comfortable doing so with limited or even no support.
- **Technology Improvement** - The convergence and improvements in technology means that a B2B platform offers a comparable customer experience similar to what is occurring on a retail eCommerce site such as Wayfair or Carrefour.
- **Shifting roles** - Sales team's responsibilities are evolving from a purely transactional role to a broader sales engagement role.

More recently post pandemic trends show that most B2B buyers actually prefer remote human interaction or digital self-service. Far from being forced to adopt digital B2B buyers are embracing it.

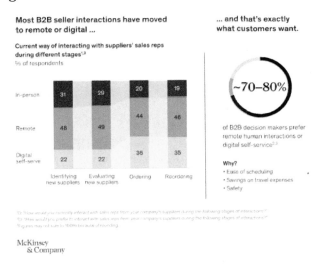

Our Consumer Behavior

As consumers, we fluidly move between the digital and physical worlds. Our commercial interactions are no different. In-person interactions are of course valuable however not every interaction needs to be in-person, nor may it be the desirable choice. This is where eCommerce and broader digital transformation efforts can and should play a larger role. For example, I have been looking at purchasing a new vehicle. My purchasing journey has taken me to the brands website, a leading online marketplace, down to the dealer for a test drive of two different models so I could understand the performance and then back onto the online marketplace. This common behavior is known as ROPO - Research Online, Purchase Offline. Before the internet and eCommerce this would have been significantly harder to do and would invariably have meant I would have come back armed with brochures to review. It was a cumbersome and time-consuming process. eCommerce and Digital have removed a significant portion of friction from the process.

Each and every business should have a digital transformation strategy. This is not a 'nice to have' - it's a necessity. A component of this should be eCommerce. Successful evaluation of your eCommerce is like any other element of business, and relies on two areas of consideration:

- **From a consumer perspective**: Does the business want to be where our consumers and shoppers are or where we want them to be?

- **From a business perspective**: Does the business want to improve efficiency, and enhance the purchasing experience for our customer partners?

Both of these should lead to the inevitable conclusion that eCommerce is an integral part of a digital transformation strategy.

Chapter 3 / Why is eCommerce different and how should you approach marketing in the digital age

CRJRO

eCommerce is different from many other channels in businesses for several reasons. The most important is that consumers engage with eCommerce sites for both information, evaluation, **and** purchase.

In the physical world, it's really hard to visit multiple stores quickly and efficiently. To evaluate pricing for example for one of your brand's goods would involve driving to and entering multiple stores. This is costly both from a time and resources perspective. So, let's take a walk down a digital aisle and see what happens......

Our walk down a digital aisle is not constrained by time, it's open 24 hours a day, seven days a week, and never closes for holidays. Shopping malls can cover thousands of square feet; however, the digital space is even larger than this with many millions of stock-keeping units on websites. Robert W. Woodruff who was a President and CEO at The Coca-Cola Company often talked about being "within an arm's reach of desire"[1]. The digital world is within a fingertips grasp of every consumer, either by laptop, tablet, or mobile device. It is well and truly ubiquitous; it is to coin the phrase 'within a fingertip's reach of desire'.

The ability of online shopping sites is that you will be shown the products you want and many other similar brands or products. This means that you can quickly digitally enter the equivalent of a Supercenter or a tiny boutique as you browse through the digital options. And in the course of fifteen minutes, you may be able to browse through the equivalent of multiple shops conveniently from your sofa.

Instead of bringing your friends along for this shopping trip to ask their opinion, there are millions of people and business associates from stores that can offer their personal recommendations. You may see visuals of their purchases in context allowing you to make a better decision. This social proof aspect of modern eCommerce has proved to be quite compelling.

As a result of this 24/7 availability, there is no need to make a decision straight away. You have the ability to make multiple visits to the same digital 'store' before you make a final purchase decision due to the ease of access of eCommerce. You may also be able to 'save' the purchases for later. Contrast this with a brick-and-mortar-only experience where there is less choice and noticeably less information.

There has been a seismic shift in our buying behavior **and** what we are exposed to. We are now confronted with a veritable deluge of marketing messages and buying options. Some of these may be even tailored based on our previous searches in an attempt to make them more relevant.

It's clear then that the consumer journey that your consumers take when buying products has been irrevocably changed. But what does this change look like? What form does it take?

There are many ways to describe customer journeys. The most common is the 'purchase funnel' or 'marketing funnel'. These terms both describe a series of logical and potentially sequential steps that consumers move through before buying a product. This does make it easier for marketers as we believe our role is to move consumers through the funnel. Fundamentally I believe that this doesn't take into account human behavior. In his book "Why People Buy: The Science of Shopping[2], the author Paco Underhill notes that shoppers are susceptible to impressions and information they acquire in stores. I would advance that the same is true of online or any retail environment for that matter.

The teams over at Google recently concluded a study that I believe represents how consumers behave online. The study named 'Decoding Decisions: The Messy Middle of Purchase Behavior' highlights this change and presents a new model[3]. The reflection that purchase behavior is messy and doesn't fit neatly into clearly defined buckets may make one feel uncomfortable, but it is an accurate reflection of the current state. Typically, in marketing we have referred to marketing as either being 'above the line' or 'below the line'. Above the line refers to the types of marketing activities that are focused on mass reach such as television, radio, print media, billboards, and cinema. Below the line refers to promotional activities that target specific individuals or a narrower target audience. This would be mediums such as direct mail, email marketing, and experiential marketing. The term above or below the line refers to where they would be in a profit and loss statement.

Typically, above-the-line marketing involves significant budgeted investment levels and are shown above a company's net profit line. Whilst this may seem a useful explanation it reflects an approach that ignores how digital marketing has transformed the media landscape. Digital marketing can be considered both above the line and below the line depending on the specific strategies and channels chosen. Historically media choice for above-the-line and to a lesser extent below the line was about carefully planned and executed bursts of activity.

The advent and efficiency of digital means of advertising has meant the strategic approach has changed to an Always on Approach. This reflects continuous and consistent marketing efforts aimed at maintaining a brand presence, engaging with customers, and driving ongoing results. This approach resonates with the model proposed by Google which reflects the need for consistent and continuous marketing efforts. It recognizes the fact that the digital world has changed the way consumers interact with media. The model proposed by Google is the following[4]:

Above: Google Marketing Model

Exposure

Consumers are exposed constantly to many varied messages both visual and text. Digital marketing experts believe this could be between 4,000 to 10,000 messages a day[5]. Not all of these have the same value for consumers, but exposure represents the sum total of all advertising from a category that you've seen or heard in all environments. Therefore, it could be in the physical world but also in the digital world. That is what always-on marketing is and organizations marketing efforts should reflect that. This is always changing and will be influenced by new messaging, but also new inputs. These can take any form from ads on Facebook to user-generated content on TikTok to ratings and reviews on sites such as Walmart or Screwfix.

Exploration and Evaluation

The representation of this loop of behavior as a continuous loop is very relevant. Decision-making is often an iterative process where consumers spend time reviewing options to make a decision. This is not uniform for all categories of products, nor does it happen exclusively online or offline. Choosing a box of cereal may require far less evaluation and exploration than buying a new car or choosing a new vacuum cleaner. The latter two examples will have a much longer exploration and evaluation loop where the features and benefits are compared to arrive at the right choice, and even then, the actual purchase may be delayed after that.

It is for this very reason that eCommerce is a domain that is not only about transactions. Consumers use eCommerce pages to not only compare prices but **compare everything**. Consumers will use these pages to compare features, and benefits, extract popular opinions from reviews, obtain information, and educate themselves. These pages form the basis for both inspiration and demonstration. This means that the role of eCommerce pages is to provide consumers with as much information as needed to assist them to move through this cycle as quickly as possible, from browsing to conversion.

Experience

Experiences consumers have with products and services form the basis of consumer recall. It can be cued or uncued but these experiences are fundamental to building associations with the brand. These experiences are not compartmentalized by the action the consumer takes. For example, a great store experience can be tainted by a poor delivery experience. The challenge in the digital age we find ourselves in now is that with a wide variety of available choices at the fingertip of desire. Equally, their poor experience might be reflected in poor reviews or negative comments on social media.

A real-life example of Google's model in action

As highlighted earlier in this chapter I am in the market for a new car. So how has the process worked in practicality? I am currently a hatchback driver of a well-known brand. I appreciate that the world is moving to Sports Utility Vehicles (SUV's) mainly as a result of their advantageous driving position and view of the road. Therefore, I started with researching what SUV models were out there as this is the direction, I was headed in. I did this online of course as it was totally impractical for me to go to all the dealerships to review the options. An online marketplace allows me to do this very efficiently. This would be the 'exploration' phase highlighted in the above model. Once I had done this, I now had numerous brands that I could choose from. Too many for me in reality. So now I had to 'evaluate' them. I proceeded to then eliminate brands that I subjectively didn't like. More than likely this was as a result of their lack of marketing efforts that I had been exposed to, rather than an arbitrary process. So now I have a shortlist of brands that I do want to purchase from. Now it was back to the 'exploration' phase for me, as I still had far more choices than could reasonably make a shortlist. So, my next step was to use publicly available data to reduce the options based on past sales information. After all, my hypothesis is that insurance companies are known to increase premiums of vehicles if they haven't sold many items.

This is because it affects spare parts availability as they age, and the probability of repairs increases. This helped me to reduce the choices to a more manageable four options which was still significant, so it's back to the 'evaluation' phase. The criteria here was model recency. When last was a new model bought, as this would give me an indication of possible changes in resale value. You may recognize the process I have gone through if you have been through it yourself. This is why I subscribe to the Google model as it represents consumer behavior and importantly in my view represents the non-linear reality of decision-making. This is an important distinction to make. The implication of non-linear decision-making **and** the sheer volume of advertising messages demands a different marketing approach, one that is suitable for the digital age.

A new marketing approach for the Digital Age

As marketing has transitioned to the digital age several noticeable elements are different from the pre-digital days. These are:

Content Intense Environment

Traditional marketing thrives on content. After all, billboards, in-store point of sale, and television adverts all have content. However, the demands from a content perspective are vastly increased. Social media algorithms differ by platform and are constantly adjusted over time. However conventional wisdom suggests that[6]:

- Instagram Feed posts: 48 hours

- Instagram Stories: 24 hours

- Instagram Reels: 14 days +

- Facebook Post: 5 hours

- YouTube Video: 30 days +

- TikTok: minutes, unless viral

- Twitter Post: 15-20 minutes

- Pinterest Pin: 6 months – 1 year

- Blog Post: 1 year +

The practice is to reuse the content in digital marketing across platforms, however the short shelf life of content elements means that the demand for fresh content is significantly higher than for traditional media.

A plethora of choice

In the pre-digital era, consumers had choices. However, they were limited by three factors, availability, cost, and distance.

Availability of media options was limited to above-the-line media such as radio, print media, billboards, and television. Below-the-line media was typically sponsorship, trade shows, and in-store media. These have literally exploded with various new formats entering. Print Media exists but circulation figures are dramatically reduced, and all print media publications now have digital equivalents. Radio has been disrupted by streaming audio by the likes of Spotify. Television has been disrupted by streaming, diluting viewership numbers and challenging funding models.

From a cost perspective, much has changed for all parties. In the pre-digital era, pretty much standard rate cards existed with discounts for volume. This inevitably favored more established brands who had both the budgets and brands to cut through, as this was expensive. Cost in the digital age is defined by a different set of rules. Budgets can be capped and can range from $1000 or less to really large budgets. Auctions are common for media inventory. This means that brands now have more control over budgets and can spend as little or as much as they want. Here's an example of how this works.

On the retail site ACME Inc advertisers participate in an auction to display their ads. Advertisers create campaigns with specific targeting criteria, and bids represent the maximum amount they're willing to pay. ACME Inc determines the available ad slots based on website traffic and user engagement. Using a combination of bid amount and ad quality, winners are selected. The winning ads are displayed on the website, and advertisers are charged based on impressions or clicks. Throughout the campaign, advertisers can optimize their bids and targeting. ACME Inc provides detailed reports and bills advertisers accordingly. This auction system ensures fair competition, maximizes revenue, and delivers targeted ads to users.

Proximity

The dimension of proximity is the one that has transformed the most with the onset of the digital era. Pre-digital media most media types required *you* as the consumer to go to them. You turned on the television and depending on the channel and the show watched an advertisement that had been scheduled often weeks in advance to appear in that slot. As a consumer, you drove past a billboard either in your own vehicle or on public transport. You were exposed to the same billboard often numerous times. Similarly, magazines and newspapers were purchased, and advertising was targeted again based on broad readership profiles.

The advent of digital has changed significantly *where* engagement with consumers or shoppers takes place. Take a typical morning for some of us. It may involve reading news or browsing social media sites over breakfast or on public transport. Or it may be during a quick coffee or lunch break that you browse on your mobile. You may switch back to your laptop or tablet if you are in front of them. Many of these sites are highly predicated on driving engagement with the target audience. It's highly measurable and by comparison to traditional marketing, highly targeted. You will constantly be served advertising that may reflect your past browsing behavior. With digital media, audiences can be segmented and targeted to achieve a laser focus. This is one of many significant differences from traditional media.

The rise of mobile

The advent of mobile devices transformed not only communications but commerce as well. Early mobile devices were mainly used as communications, however as smartphones gained in penetration so did the ability to use them for other functions. Smartphones have meant applications (apps) have been built to replicate the normal desktop experience and provide the ability to purchase wherever, whenever and, however. This means there are lower barriers to entry shopping online and consequently eCommerce has flourished. In fact, more than 2/3rds of all eCommerce is conducted on mobile devices as indicated below.

Retail Mcommerce Sales Share Worldwide, by Region, 2023
% of total retail ecommerce sales

Region	%
Asia-Pacific	80.3%
Middle East & Africa	67.8%
Southeast Asia*	66.4%
Latin America	61.9%
Western Europe	47.9%
North America	43.0%
Central & Eastern Europe	41.4%
Worldwide	67.7%

Note: includes products or services ordered using the Internet via mobile devices, regardless of the method of payment or fulfillment; includes sales on tablets; excludes travel and event tickets, payments such as bill pay, taxes, or money transfers, restaurant sales, food services and drinking place sales, gambling and other vice goods sales; *Southeast Asia is a subset of Asia-Pacific and the Southeast Asia figures are also included in the Asia-Pacific totals
Source: eMarketer, Dec 2022

281294   eMarketer | InsiderIntelligence.com

This has meant that marketing and eCommerce have become inextricably intertwined as both occur literally on the same device often within seconds or minutes of each other. This is in contrast to how these activities occurred previously, in separate locations.

The implications for marketing

The implications for marketing and digital commerce are several and call for a compelling rethink of how we delineate the areas within our businesses. There is no clear dividing line between marketing areas and commerce areas. Many large brands will see more visitors visiting their brand stores on Amazon than their own websites. Significantly due to the digital era being 'At the fingertips of desire', there is now the opportunity to seamlessly transition from marketing message to purchase at the click of a button.

This means that CEOs and C-Suite leaders need to embrace a new digital paradigm. There are two questions I would pose to you. "Would you like to engage with your consumers and shoppers at a time and place convenient for them?". If the answer to this question is 'yes', then you need to embrace eCommerce. "Does our business want to enable shoppers to purchase seamlessly once they have been exposed to marketing messages?". Once again if the answer is 'yes' then eCommerce is the route for your business. In this new digital paradigm, shoppers are exposed to marketing messages constantly at their fingertips. This means that as leaders we need to understand that engagement and purchase can and do happen in exactly the same place and this will transform purchasing behavior for years to come.

Chapter 4 / The eCommerce Amplification Effect

☙

C-Suite Leaders will notice that as eCommerce starts to grow in a business the status quo may be challenged by eCommerce and digital leaders. I call this 'The eCommerce Amplification Effect'. This is where the traditional rules of doing business are challenged and more is asked of the business covering everything from data availability to specific assortment for eCommerce retailers. This creates uncomfortable conversations inside businesses and frustration with retailers who lament the slow progress the company is making. However, none of this is new. Every retailer will ask for a differentiated assortment (and pricing), after all, differentiation in assortment makes them more distinctive to their shopper base. Every retailer will look for different promotions and different in-store executions compared to their peers. And your teams have needed to have accurate data for a long period of time too.

eCommerce will challenge many existing processes and capabilities, **amplifying** the need for much-needed transformation in your business. This will cover many areas of the business including marketing, information technology, legal, fulfillment, planning, and your go-to-market strategy. This will inevitably be reflected by your team members involved in eCommerce as it is the backbone of the way business is conducted. But why does this happen and what should you be doing about it?

Accurate data on web pages is the foundation of eCommerce

The web page that you see for a product contains many fields of data. These will include dimensions, weight, ingredient statements, country of origin, allergens, and whether it needs batteries to name just a few. These are the descriptions that a shopper sees, not your internal description, features, benefits, and several images. All of this can then be multiplied by the countries the product is sold in and the languages they require. To have a product sold on Amazon or Allegro for example you may need 150+ data fields filled in. Multiply this by the hundreds of products your company will sell on a retailer, and you have a significant data need. Differing retailers may also ask for additional fields depending on their own requirements, and the business needs for data become staggering. Usually, the composite of the data requirement is stored in many different locations in the business, thus complicating the challenge. To add further complexity there could be a material risk to your business by not having this data accurately maintained.

Imagine this scenario, your business sells hand creams. A shopper goes to Walmart looking for a basic hand cream. They look online for one and specifically look at the ingredients, as they are allergic to parabens. The allergy results in a nasty unsightly rash and they know they have a wedding this weekend to attend. The shopper clicks on Add to Basket and then gets the product later the same day. The same shopper opens the cream and lathers it on, only to find they break out in an unsightly rash. Surprised they check the package only to find to their dismay that it contains parabens. As a result of poor data management, the business could find it faces a public relations challenge as the same shopper posts on social media or depending on the instance, instigates legal action.

In reality, what presents is a master data governance challenge with the accompanying need for data quality management. This is not an eCommerce challenge, but a business challenge with potential reputational and legal risk. eCommerce is merely **amplifying** the need and unfulfilled requirements. There is of course a significant upside to gaining control of your enterprise data, with benefits realized from procurement, planning, and forecasting.

Radical Transparency and its Consequences

eCommerce has brought with it, radical transparency. When go-to-market strategies were first executed, auditing stores to evaluate pricing and assortment meant a store visit. And even then, it was fallible, after all, you can't visit all the stores in the country you were in. So, companies sprang up that offered this as a service, but this came with limitations. Usually in the form of timeliness. Digital technologies have dramatically changed this.

For shoppers, they have the ability to now do digital store visits and of course, there is Google Shopping. Between these two, shoppers are very quickly able to evaluate stores from an assortment point of view to pinpoint the product they are looking for. And then there is pricing. Pricing is now transparent, and shoppers can quickly determine whether you have the best price in real-time. The rest for shoppers is a trade-off between speed, convenience, familiarity, and cost.

For retailers, radical transparency comes through competitive analysis. Sophisticated retailers make use of web-scraping services. Web scraping involves employing a service that goes to every webpage and extracts the data on that web page. It is used to gather product information, pricing, promotions, and of course assortment. It's the foundation of retail price comparison. Various specialized tools automate this process. And because of automation, these can be set to run on any day of the week, at any time, and even multiple times of the day.

This means that for retailers when virtually anything can be searched for/scraped off the internet, distinctiveness becomes a real requirement. After all, the price they display is publicly accessible to anyone using the internet, and the features and benefits are easily displayed. This means the focus and evolution of the retail offering needs to come from elsewhere and needs to constantly evolve to stay ahead of what can be digitally gleaned. This is both a threat and an opportunity for retailers. This is also where omnichannel retailers can accentuate and blend their in-store capabilities with their digital capabilities to enhance their distinctiveness in the eyes of shoppers. Usually, these shoppers may also spend more than either eCommerce only or brick and mortar only shoppers.

For manufacturers of goods, this means that the retailer you are selling through knows or can very quickly work out what assortment you are providing to others and what the pricing is. For businesses like Amazon, this is one of the foundations of its business model. Amazon automatically matches pricing in the market using web scraping technology. But its internal processes are different from traditional retailers. In a traditional retailer, a lower price requires human input to change the price. In Amazon it doesn't, the system does it and then your teams will be the recipients of communication that the price of your product has changed. If Amazon is impacted by this change it may raise claims for costs.

The reality is that in this era of radical transparency, retailers need differentiation in an assortment from you. When shoppers can easily pass over a retailer for someone with better pricing or faster shipping the need for differentiation becomes more pressing. There are two ways to achieve this, through their own private label or with your assistance. It's a Hobson's choice for manufacturers, but one they need to face.

Transparency is not an eCommerce issue, it's a business issue. Retailers want differentiation, this has been true long before eCommerce exploded. It's only now that your eCommerce teams understand this and are raising it, that it seems like an eCommerce issue, but it's been there all along. This is how radical transparency manifests and **amplifies** the need for all businesses, both brand owners and retailers to look at differentiation and distinctiveness.

Commercial Policy

Commercial policies are the rebates, terms, conditions, pricing, and promotions the business uses as part of its go-to-market strategy. This is often referred to as the total customer investment. The principle behind commercial policies is that they should be fair, and equitable and drive the right behavior amongst commercial partners. Maturity in this area varies substantially. Some companies have a set of principles that are in many cases historical in nature and are repeated year after year. In other companies, these policies use a common language and approach for the investment and have clearly defined parameters. They will have clearly defined promotion length and depth parameters based on analytics to determine the right level of discounting. These will then be implemented across the market/s that the business operates in.

As alluded to earlier, digital and eCommerce have brought with them an era of radical transparency. The same applies to a business's commercial policy. As eCommerce grows in a business, teams will highlight that a customer like Amazon has a price that the team feels that they possibly shouldn't be able to achieve, given the cost price given to them. In many cases this is true. But this ignores the business model and technology these companies have adopted. Businesses like Amazon have adopted an approach to pricing called 'dynamic pricing' or 'repricing'. This is where the business dynamically reprices the product it is selling automatically based on inputs it receives.

This will often be referred to as a business such as Amazon as 'setting the market price'. According to Andrea K. Leigh[1] a ten-year former Amazon Category leader, and a prominent educator and writer in the field of eCommerce, Amazon is a 'price follower'. This is as a result of its repricing approach. What the pricing highlights is that there is a price in the market that a business like Amazon can reprice against. I refer to this as the 'leaky bucket' of commercial policy.

There is a 'leak' and a price is out in the market and it could potentially be dilutive to the business margin and revenue. In a digital age, with new retail players, there is a need to evolve and improve the implementation and execution of commercial policies to reflect the new realities. These could take the form of cart limiters, depth of promo discounts, specific language in distributor contracts or prohibit reselling.

eCommerce Amplification

There is a clear case for eCommerce **amplifying** the need for business evolution and transformation. It's the symptom of a business challenge, not the cause. eCommerce has merely shone the spotlight on elements of business practice that have been present for a long time, but haven't evolved with technology. So, what should you be doing about this?

- ☑ Digital transformation is not only the eCommerce team's responsibility, it's a business imperative, to ensure every department has a digital transformation strategy
- ☑ Establish the root cause of requests that emanate from digital & eCommerce teams, then address the internal ways of working to more efficiently go to market
- ☑ Include digital questions or digital elements in all planning processes across functions including Supply Chain, R&D etc. to trigger discussions about eCommerce-specific needs

Chapter 5 / A Primer on eCommerce Go To Market Strategy

❧

Determining your routes to market and routes to the consumer is integral to your business's success. When designing a route-to-market strategy it's important to understand the different elements of each route-to-market and be able to make choices. Michael Porter in 1996 said that "Strategy is about making choices, trade-offs; it's about deliberately choosing to be different[1]."

For this reason, we must understand the role that each eCommerce channel or business model plays in a go-to-market strategy. By understanding the choices, and therefore the trade-offs that are needed, businesses can make the right choices for their particular situation. It's clear that companies that win in the consumer packaged goods (CPG) or fast-moving consumer goods (FMCG) space have a clearly defined channel strategy.

They understand the development of these channels over time and align their business efforts behind this. They develop accurate forecasts of growth rates, and cost-to-serve and also understand the considerations for each channel. eCommerce channels are no different.

Total Commerce Strategy

One of the first choices any business will need to evaluate is whether to adopt a Total Commerce Strategy or not. A Total Commerce Strategy is one where a business chooses to be where its customers are *and* controls the execution at the point of purchase. This comes with implications, particularly when considering eCommerce channels. Operating in eCommerce channels requires businesses to have the capability to operate in these channels which means that recruitment will be necessary. Alternatively, there is the choice not to engage in eCommerce channels. However, this equally has repercussions. There will be businesses or self-employed individuals who choose to sell on your behalf on these channels. There is no right or wrong approach here, it's merely a choice of how one approaches the market.

When considering the approach for your route-to-market strategy it's important to have several considerations in mind:

A Consumers Perspective - Consumer Centricity

When designing any route-to-market strategy it's important to orientate the business from the consumer's perspective. Earlier in the book we discussed how consumers fluidly move between the digital and physical landscapes. This is completely natural and happens daily. Equally, consumers move between channels and don't make the distinctions between channels that are common in industries. It is quite conceivable that in the space of a few hours, consumers will order an item on Instacart and then shortly after walk into a large supermarket to begin their shopping. Later the same consumer may peruse ratings and reviews on Amazon before deciding to purchase an item in another store altogether.

It is quite common (and understandable) for businesses and management within businesses to look after their particular channels and in turn the customers within their channels. However, routes to market are essentially routes to consumers. It's therefore important when creating a channel strategy regardless of whether it is for offline or online channels that the perspective of the consumer is paramount in this. This is often referred to as customer-centricity. Gartner defines Customer Centricity[2] as:

"Customer centricity is the ability of people in an organization to understand customers' situations, perceptions, and expectations. Customer centricity demands that the customer is the focal point of all decisions related to delivering products, services, and experiences to create customer satisfaction, loyalty, and advocacy."

The approach taken should reflect as much competitive intelligence and insight that can be garnered about your key customers buying behavior to inform their channel usage and in turn the route to market strategy. This means you will sell the products and the services relevant to the customer when they are shopping in the channel. These offerings will address the distinct needs of each customer group. Sometimes this may be convenient and speedy delivery like Amazon Prime can deliver and in other cases, this will be a more informed counter service offering that another retailer provides. Ideally, this process of ensuring customer centricity is conducted through a process of market mapping, identifying common attributes, and buying behavior to segment on potential performance.

The balance between market penetration and control

Bear in mind that a Total Commerce Strategy, one where a business makes use of all channels has consequences. A mix of channels can result in potential channel conflict, possible margin erosion, and dissatisfied trading partners. Add the online channels into this mix and the challenge is magnified. However, this is not magnified due to online channels being price makers in the market, when in fact, many aren't. It is magnified due to transparency, digitally native players like Amazon who use technology to match pricing in the market already, this will be covered in more detail later.

To stay in control both online and offline you need to identify these potential risks and have an approach to deal with them. The business can limit the channels and sell less, it depends on the category and products you deal with as to what the preferable strategy is. A further option could be to adjust the SKU selection by channel to reduce cross-channel conflict.

Another option is to seek market coverage, in order to establish the brand and its products as the 'accepted standard' by getting the product in front of as many customers as possible. The consequence of doing this is that there is a loss of control as all partners carry the brand. In addition, it can be difficult to build relationships with partners when there is no significant difference between them.

The equilibrium between channel profitability & growth

When evaluating your route-to-market strategy it's important to maintain the balance between channel profitability and growth. We've established earlier that eCommerce is a growing channel. This is mainly due to new digital buyers. It's important to note that these new digital buyers may not be entirely new to your business or in the categories you participate in. Many of them could well be buyers who bought through brick-and-mortar channels and are now transitioning to buying at least some of their purchases through digital channels. Therefore, it's important to look at the complete channel landscape and balance the growth achieved through eCommerce channels with the growth achieved in other channels. Naturally, the question should be asked about channel profitability as this may not all be incremental growth.

eCommerce channels should have a very clear growth channel objective with a clear path to profitability over the short to medium term. We will cover the nature of marketplaces and their impact on channel dynamics; suffice it to say that expanding onto eCommerce channels like marketplaces can bring you into conflict with your existing retailers who themselves see the growth that is possible on marketplaces as an opportunity.

In the following chapters, we will cover the nature of the different routes to market, the implications of each, and the considerations for brand owners.

CHAPTER 6 / Omnichannel

ೞೲ

What is omnichannel retailing?

This is typically where a business transacts through more than one 'channel' of business. omnichannel retailing is a form of business to consumer (B2C) eCommerce as described in Chapter 1. This term is often used to describe businesses that have a physical store/s and an online business operating alongside the physical one. These businesses offer consumers the ability to choose where and how they interact with the retailer to maximize the consumer experience. The business will ensure that the consumer can interact with the multiple sales and media channels whilst retaining their information as they move seamlessly between them. For retailers, this means operating across purchases in-store, purchases on a desktop device, tablet, and mobile devices. This is no simple task for retailers and many need to implement significant investments to facilitate consumer interactions across the channels. Significant upgrades need to be made to retailers' sales, supply chain, and information technology systems to facilitate these orders.

As this model is about deciding where and how consumers interact with the business, many will also offer the ability to transact online but choose the location of the fulfillment of the order, either in-store or at a specified address. The aim from a consumer perspective is a unified consumer experience agnostic of the channel. Examples of prominent omnichannel retailers are Walmart, Ahold Delhaize, Costco, Carrefour, and Ikea.

How do these retailers operate?

These retailers operate both retail stores and online stores. They will take customers' orders in both these environments. In the physical store, the shopper decides what products they want from the aisles which are typically laid out according to a predefined floor plan. The consumer then checks out at a check out either self-checkout or assisted. In the digital environment, consumers place orders online themselves either by searching for items, using favorites (typically grocery), or browsing through the online catalog.

Considerations for omnichannel retailers

Harmonized real-time inventory

Retailers over time have realized that inventory is needed to optimize working capital and effectively manage distributed store inventory. A diverse store network will forecast individual store sales by item and then consolidate this into an enterprise-wide demand plan to operate with. Historically this has only really needed to be done on a daily basis. At the end of the operating day when the close procedures for each store are done there would be a sales file reconciliation that returns to the head office the sales of each store which would then be deducted from the stock-holding to reflect the current inventory position.

However, eCommerce has added an extra dimension to this for retailers. A typical scenario for an omnichannel retailer of a consumer walking into the store and picking up an item off the shelf. With an online store, the same product could be selected by an online shopper. This can create a situation that the single item left could be 'bought' by the online shopper and then picked up by an in-store shopper shortly thereafter. To account for an accurate stock count and ensure that *both* consumers are happy, retailers need to move from a daily (or less frequent) reconciliation of their inventory position to achieve this in real-time. This is needed for several reasons:

- Avoid stock-outs.

- Enhanced customer experience.

- Manage inventory levels.

- Meet delivery schedules more easily.

This is clearly a transformative shift for retailers and one that requires a significant investment in ERP systems. It's also a significant capital project for most retailers. Alternatives to this investment do exist, with Instacart being the most noticeable business model to solve this issue. Instacart uses sophisticated prediction models to determine what the probable inventory is based on past sales history accompanied by a daily provision of available inventory. Real-time inventory enables eCommerce and allows the retailer to offer a seamless consumer experience but represents a substantial investment in both information technology infrastructure and business processes. Real-time inventory has benefits beyond eCommerce enablement but is a necessary prerequisite for a successful omnichannel business.

Fulfillment

The fulfillment process is often one which poses significant challenges for retailers. A traditional approach has the goods being picked up in stores by shoppers, this of course makes it a lot easier for retailers to control the environment and the quality of the goods.

In eCommerce fulfillment, there are many considerations for retailers to navigate:

- **Temperature and the cold chain** - If operating a business that has chilled or frozen items, operators need to ensure that they pick, deliver, and maintain the products at the correct temperature. This is so that the cold chain is maintained, and the product is not spoiled. This will often mean separate storage if doing so from a store or in a separate compartment/s in a delivery vehicle.

- **Fresh and Short-life Goods** - When operating a retail outlet where fresh and short-shelf-life products are, the shopper takes responsibility for selecting the items. In an eCommerce fulfillment environment, the retailers and their staff take responsibility for this task. This means that sufficient training needs to take place to ensure that staff members pick the freshest items to avoid costly returns or refusals.

- **Maintaining Food Safety** - eCommerce dramatically increases the handling of products and magnifies the risk for retailers. In a grocery environment, different goods are packed together so the risk of product damage resulting in leakage and spillage multiplies.

- **Bulky items** - Items that are bulky or awkward can make it challenging for retailers. In some cases, they can't be handled by one person resulting in additional people resources necessary to ensure fulfillment. Bulky items may also present an additional damages concern due to their size given the additional handling that comes within the eCommerce value chain.

- **Outer Packaging** - Packaging is often not suitable for the handling that happens in eCommerce deliveries. Many retailers will request stronger outer boxes and 'Ships in Own Container' (SIOC) to reduce costs.

- **Volumetric Weight** - Also known as dimensional weight, is a calculation used in logistics to determine the weight of a package based on its size rather than its physical weight. By considering both weight and size logistics companies ensure they are accurately compensated for the capacity used by a package.

For retailers, there are several considerations when designing a fulfillment method for their online operation. Firstly, there is no one size fits all model when it comes to fulfillment. Many retailers have both urban and rural stores. And there may be more than one store servicing a limited geography. This means that retailers may not need to transform all stores in an area for eCommerce fulfillment.

Types of omnichannel fulfillment models

In-store fulfillment

In-store fulfillment is one of the most common methods that retailers who have stores use. There are several reasons for this:

- It allows them to leverage existing stores, and existing store staff with limited additional capital outlay.

- It's a low-investment model that enables the retailer to have a member of staff pick items located in the store.

- It's relatively quick for stores to launch, as the investment will be needed in picking carts and handsets, but these can be relatively easily procured.

- It's close to the final delivery destination, usually being residential homes.

- The localized store assortment can be accommodated by providing a similar experience to the in-store assortment, which is beneficial for shoppers.

This system works with retail staff who pick up the order from the same shelves used by offline shoppers. Staff have handsets telling them which products to pick. If products are unavailable, the handset suggests substitutions usually informed by purchasing behavior. Orders are usually consolidated at the back of the store. The primary point of picking the order is always the fixture and staff will typically follow a predetermined route through the store to pick as efficiently as possible. There are several challenges when it comes to this model for retailers:

- By comparison to other models, in-store fulfillment can be slower as typically between 50-100 items can be picked per hour per person.[1]

- Order accuracy may be lower.

- Limited Scalability as it relies on human contractors.

- Assortment and order capacity is constrained by the store's space.

- The presence of retail staff picking orders in the same physical space as shoppers can detract from the experience for shoppers.

- In-store picking can impact the availability of products for shoppers as the picking may deplete stock before replenishment can take place.

- If a store has a high concentration of eCommerce orders this can impact the demand pattern for the store, necessitating a change to staff rosters.

Centralized or eCommerce fulfillment centers

Another form of fulfillment is to centralize eCommerce orders and supply through an eCommerce fulfillment center. An eCommerce fulfillment center is normally purpose-built for picking multiple individual orders. This would normally be a separate distribution center from the retailer's store fulfillment center. To replenish physical stores, retailers typically optimize for both slow and fast-moving items but ship to stores in partial or full pallet loads.

In an eCommerce distribution center, retailers are optimizing for picking individual orders. This normally involves extensive use of automation and conveyor belt systems to speed up the picking and packing process. In some cases, technology companies such as the Ocado Group and Autostore are making use of robotics, automation, and artificial intelligence to significantly reduce labor costs. These types of fulfillment centers are often referred to as Automated Customer Fulfillment Centers (CFCs). There are several reasons that this may be a preferable solution for retailers:

- Faster picking and lower labor costs vs. an in-store picking approach.

- Decoupling the assortment from the store provides an opportunity for retailers to offer a broader assortment.

- Increased capacity to deliver online orders.

- Order picking is removed from the store reducing in-store congestion.

- Centralized fulfillment can make it easier to manage slow-moving lines and forecast more accurately, particularly on perishable items.

This model will typically have three sections in the distribution center, an ambient, chilled, and frozen section. The orders are received centrally by the distribution center, picked, and then delivered by pooling orders with a geographic area to optimize the routing of vehicles. There are several challenges that retailers may experience in operating this model:

- There is a significant upfront capital investment, particularly when considering robotics and automation.

- It can be difficult to scale automated distribution centers.

- Due to the upfront capital investment and accompanying depreciation, the utilization of the distribution center needs to scale quickly in order to not impact the P&L.

- In retail stores there would be the opportunity to clear slow-moving stock via mark-downs, in centralized fulfillment centers this opportunity does not exist.

Micro-fulfillment centers

Micro-fulfillment centers (MFCs) are designed to support the eCommerce orders at a store level. These fulfillment centers either make use of existing space in the store or are attached to the stores. These MFCs are used to overcome some of the limitations of in-store fulfillment. These are designed to support a smaller geographic radius than CFCs and are in close proximity to shoppers. These are popular with retailers for the following reasons:

- Co-location can repurpose unused or underperforming existing space with a store.

- It utilizes existing replenishment processes and also reduces network transportation costs.

- Adding automation and robotics to the model will slash operational expenses and improve profitability.

- They are ideally suited to urban and suburban areas as there is sufficient order density to make this model work well.

The method of operation is very similar to a CFC. Orders are received and prioritized and fulfilled through delivery processes to consumers' homes. As this fulfillment model typically serves urban and suburban areas, the MFC will mean that other stores will not necessarily have to offer delivery, as the MFC will cover multiple stores' operating needs. However, like all models, there are challenges in this particular fulfillment model. These are:

- Unpredictable consumer demand is harder to manage with a decentralized stock model, MFCs are designed for predictable demand and normal demand patterns.

- The impact of stock-outs is magnified in a decentralized inventory model possibly impacting customer experience.

- SKU proliferation typically drives volume and overall experiences, but more SKUs equals a less profitable MFC.

- It is very challenging to balance inventory between the physical store and the MFC.

Third-party fulfillment

The use of third parties has enabled many retailers to offer an online capability quickly with little direct investment. This method normally involves passing a store-level stock file on a daily or more frequent basis to a third party. The third party will have an online presence where shoppers can order, check out, pay, and then track their orders. Examples of these are Instacart, Uber Eats, and Deliveroo.

These third-party platforms typically take the order and then send it to the driver or rider to fulfill. This driver or rider is often not a paid employee of the company but a contractor. The contractor delivers the order on behalf of the platform. The third-party fulfillment provider charges the retailer a commission for appearing on the platform. Items that are shown online in these models may be at a higher price than the retailer's own stores to cover the cost of fulfillment. This is a preferred method for some retailers because:

- Least amount of investment.

- Fast realization of online presence in the market.

- Can be useful to test demand for a later expansion of the retailer's own platforms.

- The third parties are often digital experts with an advanced website, app, and routing capability.

There is a limitation of this model, however. I refer to this model as a *'geographically constrained order density model'*. This is because to realize a reasonable level of profitability the platform operator needs as many orders within a constrained area to make it worthwhile for the driver or rider to fulfill orders. Without sufficient demand, the rider or driver can not realize a reasonable return and will withdraw their services. There will be challenges in adopting this business model

- The retailer has limited control over the shopper's experience, the platform owns all consumer data.

- The assortment is often limited to ensure availability.

- The riders or drivers are often in the store at the same time as regular shoppers, which can impact in-store shoppers.

- Differential pricing and delivery charges can impact the retailer's brand perceptions.

- There may be unintended consequences as providers often favor speed over accuracy.

The best model for retailers

To cover an entire estate of stores retailers will often adopt a hybrid model of two or more of the preceding models. There are several considerations that retailers could have in choosing the best model for themselves:

- **The size of the opportunity** - If there is rapid online growth converting more stores to in-store picking and using third-party fulfillment could provide a path to growth for retailers.

- **Population density within a target area** - This can impact the type of model as retailers could make use of a dedicated eCommerce fulfillment model such as a CFC or MFC.

- **Competitive threat** - There may be an immediate threat from a competitor, therefore offering a fast time-to-market offering could be the solution.

- **Shopper behavior** - eCommerce economics favors high average order values to cover the cost of fulfillment. Depending on the retailer's basket dynamics there will be a solution that best meets its needs.

- **Capital Cost** - With competing priorities such as refitting an existing store estate, retailers may have to delay or deploy a different model to achieve an online presence.

Types of omnichannel Delivery

There are many varied methods of delivery that retailers use to get products to their customers. The primary considerations are need, cost, and flexibility for both parties. Many retailers may offer a combination of one or more of these methods for several reasons

- **Customer preference**: Depending on need, shoppers will trade off cost for speed. Offering multiple versions allows shoppers to trade off one for the other.

- **Product type**: Not all products need to be shipped quickly. Perishables for example do need quick delivery, furniture can be shipped over a longer time period.

- **Location:** Depending on where the shopper is can determine the delivery method. More rural locations for example may not be feasible to be reached quickly.

Click and Collect

In this method, the shopper buys the product online and then goes to the store to collect the item. This is referred to as 'click and collect' or 'Buy online pick-up in store' (BOPIS) There are several variations of this model that retailers have implemented. There are variations on this which are usually due to location. There is the click-and-collect operating from existing delivery vehicles with canopies in car parks, or standalone pick-up areas. There may also be in-store pick-up, both automated (Walmart) and not automated. The predominantly French model of 'Drive' stores where shoppers go to a purpose-built facility to pick up goods (Auchan, LeClerc, Carrefour). In the 'Drive' model the items are brought to your vehicle by a staff member. Curbside pickup is the predominantly North American equivalent of the format where specific places are reserved near the front of the store for vehicles to pick up. The retailers may offer the facility of having their staff to deliver the items to the vehicle.

Some retailers have worked to utilize either existing internal space or external space and provide lockers. These lockers can be opened with a unique code provided to the shopper and have the capability to store perishable, frozen, and ambient items. This method is growing more popular with retailers because:

- There are often reduced or no fees for shoppers.

- Shoppers enjoy the capability of not having to wait for items to ship.

  - Shoppers can check the order immediately and return items if things are incorrect.
  - There is a possibility of an incremental purchase and more foot traffic through the stores. Shoppers may remember that they have forgotten an item and go into to store for additional items.
  - For retailers, this leverages existing store infrastructure and personnel.
  - Depending on the retailer's technology systems Click-and-Collect can allow for pickup within the next two hours or faster, which consumers often desire.
  - Some models like lockers provide flexibility to collect at a time that's convenient to them rather than arriving for a specified slot.

This model works with shoppers browsing the online inventory and when they find an item they want, they will be given the option to select pick up, Collect from Store, Curbside Pickup, or delivery. Once the order has been placed, the local storefront will fulfill and place the order for collection according to the selected time slot for customer collection. However, like all models, there are considerations:

- Potential pick-up queues can diminish the shopper experience.

- Lack of inventory in the store can impact the operation.

- The entire retail team needs to be aligned to the strategy, so that they can direct shoppers and assist with additional requests such as substitutions.

- Some investment will need to be made to ensure the cold chain is maintained for perishable and frozen goods.

- These customers may not be net new to the retailer and therefore profitability needs to be considered.

Delivery to home

Home delivery was one of the first eCommerce delivery methods. This service allows customers to purchase goods and have them delivered to their homes or in some cases offices. It has the benefit that it allows retailers to reach a wider audience and sell their products to shoppers who may not be able, for whatever reason, to physically visit the store. There are several reasons why home delivery is offered by retailers:

- It's convenient for shoppers as it eliminates the need to travel to a store.

- It saves time for shoppers who can shop online and save time traveling to and from stores and picking the groceries from the store.

- Comparison shopping is easier for shoppers, as they can compare multiple sites for the best pricing easily.

So how does it work? Orders are placed online and then during the checkout phase; the shopper selects the day and time slot that suits them. Some retailers may offer same-day delivery or allow the shopper to schedule days in advance. This is often within the next week as retailers will need to honor pricing and promotions on the day the shopper placed the order so retailers will often curtail the forward booking window. The retailer will then look to collate all the orders for a geographic area. This is done to reduce the distance traveled and time needed to deliver the orders to improve efficiency and effectiveness. There are several challenges to this delivery method:

- If there are delays in delivery due to unforeseen circumstances such as traffic, this can impact the shopper experience.

- Shipping costs depending on the dimensions and weight of the product can be more expensive than picking up in person.

- Some shoppers feel that home delivery can be risky especially if purchases are left outside the home for an extended period.

- To be efficient and cost-effective the time periods available for selection may not be as preferable as click and collect.

Quick Commerce

Quick commerce, also known as on-demand delivery is a type of delivery service where purchases are delivered to shoppers on-demand usually within a very short time frame, usually within an hour or less with some operators offering this as quick as ten to fifteen minutes. This will normally be offered by a third party who will pick the items from the omnichannel retailer. These products are normally household essentials needed in an emergency. omnichannel retailers will offer this to replace convenient purchases that would be made, or to attempt to gain some additional traffic from convenience stores.

The rise of quick commerce is attributed to the increasing demand for instant gratification and convenience among consumers. Quick commerce relies heavily on sophisticated logistics networks, real-time data analytics and technology to operate. Quick commerce either operates using existing stores or makes use of 'dark stores' in close proximity to the customer base.

Recommendations for Quick Commerce

☑ Collaborate with retail partners on assortment. Quick commerce offers a limited assortment dictated to by the retailer.

☑ Define a strategy to activate on the platform for relevant occasions or missions.

☑ Determine the overlap particularly on retail media between the original retailer platform and the quick commerce platforms.

☑ Review assortments and create 'virtual' bundles with partners to increase the average order value with quick commerce platform partners.

Drone Delivery

This method refers to the use of unmanned aerial vehicles (drones) to transport packages and deliver them directly to customers' doorsteps. This method allows for speed and efficiency in the delivery process. The limited capacity of drones means this method is ideal for delivery of small lightweight packages over small to medium distances. Drones are regarded as a more cost-effective delivery solution especially for last-mile delivery, which is often the most expensive part of the process.

Widespread adoption of drones is still in the early stages. There are several considerations such as regulatory frameworks, safety management and airspace management to be considered. So how does this method work?

Order placement follows the same path to the eCommerce orders described earlier in this chapter. The drones are then loaded at the drone delivery hub. The drone then follows a predetermined flight path using GPS navigation, relying on sensors and cameras for obstacle avoidance. Once the drone reaches the delivery location it either lands or lowers the package using a winch system. In some systems this is automated but in others human assistance may be required to take delivery of the package.

Recommendations for doing business with omnichannel Retailers

In the preceding section, we covered the impact of eCommerce on retailers. It's a transformative shift driven by consumers' needs to interact with retailers however and wherever they want to. The impact is not one-sided, it is felt on both sides, with suppliers of goods to omnichannel retailers also having to re-assess their Go-to-market approach. eCommerce introduces several challenges for manufacturers and distributors of goods.

Typically, when evaluating the approach to omnichannel retail it's prudent to evaluate what percentage of the retailer's business is derived through digital channels. The approach will be different if it is 1% vs. 10%. When considering working with omnichannel retailers the following should be considered.

Commercial levers are different

The activities that translate to business success in a brick-and-mortar environment are different from those in a digital environment. In a brick-and-mortar environment, the focus is on:

- Increasing coverage and distribution of your SKUs in the store estate.

- Ensuring accuracy in pricing.

- Gaining and ensuring your fair share of the space at the primary fixture.

- Looking for additional merchandising locations throughout the store to increase the visual impact of your brands.

- Merchandising according to your category principles.

- Ensuring the right type of packaging for shelf standout.

In an omnichannel digital environment, the focus changes to:

- **Visual Content** - In a digital retail environment, visual content in the form of pack images and supporting collateral is a substitute for physical packaging, and providing content that converts browsers to buyers is important.

- **Text Content** - Similar to visual content, text content allows the supplier to provide features and benefits to convert browsers.

- **Ratings & Reviews** - If a retailer has ratings and reviews displayed on its website, shoppers will often review them to determine whether to purchase the item.

- **Search results and navigation** - In an online environment this replaces placement and optimizing the results of search is critically important. There are several factors that can influence results, such as the right product attributes, relevant descriptions to name a few.

- **Additional media opportunities** - In a similar way to an offline environment additional merchandising locations can exist online.

Not only is the focus different for these commercial levers but much of what happens in a digital retail environment is achieved through technology. The digital age has ushered in a new area called algorithmic retailing. This is where what you as a shopper see on a retailer's website is the output of an algorithm. The algorithm could be scoring your product based on how many and what quality of images you provide, and the text you provide in the form of product titles and product descriptions. Ratings and reviews and the sales velocity of your products could all factor into an algorithm that dictates which products shoppers see.

Algorithmic retail implies that suppliers of goods need to optimize for both the **online and offline** environments ensuring that the shopper gets accurate and relevant information in both locations. Retailers will increasingly look to increase both the use of and sophistication of their environments to drive more sales and higher profits whilst attaining the same level of control of the retail environment online that they have offline.

Recommendations

- ☑ Integrate the commercial levels of visibility from an eCommerce perspective into your annual rebates and commercial terms.

- ☑ Allow for and understand distribution complexities when assortment is considered focusing on ensuring your product is available should there be CFCs, MFCs, or pick from the store.

- ☑ Consider all fulfillment methods as an opportunity to extend your assortment.

☑ Understand the retailer's requirements for both visual as well as text content and deliver quality, accurate data.

☑ Understand the profitability of eCommerce from an activity-based costing perspective.

Joint business planning becomes more complex

Joint business planning (JBPs) is a process whereby retailers and suppliers of goods (manufacturer, broker, supplier, etc.) align around the goals, strategies, and action plans to deliver mutually beneficial outcomes for both parties. I have often heard CPG and Durable Goods (DG) manufacturers separate the process into an eCommerce plan and a brick-and-mortar plan. It's understandable how and why this occurs; often the teams that manage these two areas are often separate.

However, this is counterintuitive and not productive for the most important stakeholder, the shopper or consumer. After all, this is the only area where a manufacturer of goods and retailer have the same objective; capturing more shopper spend.

Earlier we highlighted that *"Customer centricity demands that the customer is the focal point of all decisions related to delivering products, services, and experiences to create customer satisfaction, loyalty, and advocacy."* This means the focus should be on the shopper at the center of joint business planning and produce a plan that caters to how this segment interacts with the retailer, be it online or offline. The implications of this for joint business planning are:

- **Shopper profiles** - Shopper profiles will need to include how and through what channels shoppers engage with the retailers. Are there differing basket sizes depending on online vs. offline usage? How is their behavior different or the same?

- **Situational assessment** - Situational analysis needs to be done for both retail environments. Are market shares for the brand the same or different online vs. offline.

- **Execution strategies** - Execution strategies will need to reflect both digital and brick-and-mortar environments, ensuring that the message reflects the objective as well as the shopping behavior.

- **Scorecards** - Ideally scorecards should include both offline and online measures to ensure that execution and implementation are tracked in both environments

- **Data availability** - Underpinning all of the joint business planning is data, and the availability of data is key to ensuring robust plans. Having the right level of data and being able to distinguish between online and offline is key.

Recommendations

☑ Collapse the internal silos during your JBP process and focus on the shopper first, not online, or offline.

☑ eCommerce teams should work closely with and/or educate omnichannel customer accounts as to what to expect during negotiations.

☑ Plan for execution in both retail environments (offline and online) to reduce incremental spending asks.

☑ Negotiate eCommerce and bricks & mortar as one fully integrated shopper-facing business.

☑ Consider what data sources that will underpin your analytics and from where they could be sourced.

Shopping behavior, in general, looks different

As CPG and Durable Goods companies, it's always tempting to believe that our brand saliency is so strong that shoppers start with the brand first. In a digital environment, we know there may be differences between categories but generally, most search is unbranded as highlighted below.

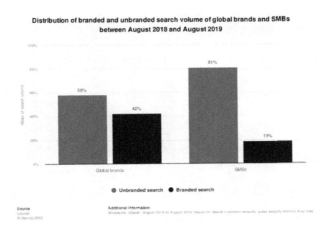

Distribution of branded and unbranded search volume of global brands and SMBs between August 2018 and August 2019

Generally, shopping behavior particularly where multiple items are required are captured on a list. There is a Twitter handle @ShoppingListTwt[2] that captures this behavior and is a reminder that brand saliency doesn't always translate to shopping behavior.

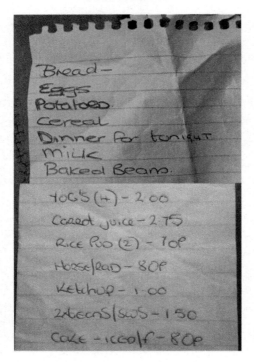

Shopping behavior as can be seen from the above is not always branded. Therefore, particularly when working with omnichannel partners on digital platforms we need to focus on doing two things:

- Optimize for the way retailer's platforms work particularly with how shoppers shop which is usually using unbranded search terms.

- Ensure that you take advantage of always-on marketing opportunities for media placement on retail platforms.

Shopping behavior has also changed where consumers shop, in many cases this could be shopping at certain retailers' stores less often and then paradoxically consolidating shopping at other retailers.

Recommendations

☑ Invest in shopper research to understand shopper behavior across both brick-and- mortar and online.

☑ Connect your shopper marketing team to the broader eCommerce team.

☑ Understand how your shoppers search for your products in 'shopper language' not the language used within your business, then adjust your content to reflect that.

☑ Create your own hypothesis of the shopper journey on your retailer's site so you can decide what messages should be communicated at what part of the journey.

Channel and Category mix impacts retail P&Ls

As explained earlier in this chapter the move to omnichannel retailing is accompanied by a need for capital investment and ongoing operating costs that weren't there in a purely brick-and-mortar business model. Many retailers are seeing a change with an increasing contribution from online. This comes with an impact on the bottom line, which from the following chart is significant.

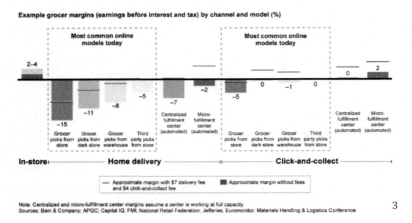

Example grocer margins (earnings before interest and tax) by channel and model (%)

Above: Grocer Margins for different fulfillment models

The implication for suppliers to omnichannel retailers is that commercial negotiations may include increased margin requirements placing pressure on the P&L of suppliers alongside their own need to increase internal capabilities (and therefore headcount).

Recommendations

☑ Explore ways to collaboratively reduce costs for both parties; supply chain, sourcing, and minimum order quantities can all be great levers

☑ Review assortment and Revenue Growth Management models to unlock growth for both parties

☑ Model your own and your retailer's P&L down to the SKU level to determine where value is gained and destroyed

Differentiation in the digital age is harder to maintain

For many years retailers have made use of competitive price intelligence, and senior leaders have been confronted by their retail colleagues with the evidence of this. This is nothing new. What has transformed this in the digital age is the ability of all large and small companies to leverage this capability. As retailers' online presence has improved so has the visibility of both their assortment and their services. This is for both shoppers and competitors. Literally, *everything* is visible. This level of transparency has meant that for retailers their ability to differentiate has become harder. Previously retailers could differentiate on price, now retailers can make use of sophisticated software to re-price goods. And certain retailers such as Amazon have built their business model around this capability.

The implication for suppliers is that retailers will begin to ask for real differentiation. And by this it won't simply be a variant or flavor, it will be a shopper discernible variant as only this will be enough to encourage shoppers to move retailers. This reduced ability to differentiate will also encourage retailers to speed up private label development as this will be one of the only ways to truly differentiate themselves from an assortment perspective. All this is normal and part of the magnification effect of eCommerce discussed earlier in the book.

Recommendations

- ☑ Innovate for channel profit, meaningful innovation that delivers better margins
- ☑ Look for meaningful innovations beyond flavor and variant that delivers value to both parties

☑ Review flexibility in your supply chain to deliver meaningful cost reductions

☑ Find meaningful innovation that seamlessly blends offline into online behavior

☑ Consider exclusives, targeted launches, or online-only early releases of products for retailers

Assortment and Portfolio Planning

Depending on the fulfillment and delivery strategy chosen by retailers there are multiple different configurations possible. There could be several different configurations underpinning the final route to the shopper picking up the product. Many brick-and-mortar retailers pick from stores and/or convert existing non-productive floor space into eCommerce Micro-fulfilment operations. This means that if you aren't in the assortment for the local store, you're not available for online delivery. These stores also become disproportionately important for your revenue contribution. In addition, an out-of-stock at the store level will translate to an out-of-stock at the online level. This then creates the next challenge for you as a brand, you will get substituted and it may not be your product. A further consideration for you is that retailers will typically only pick stock from the aisles, therefore any additional stock used to build bulk displays may not be used to service demand as this slows down the picking process making it less productive.

Recommendations

☑ Understand what your online distribution is

☑ Do you know which stores are used for fulfillment?

☑ Do you have the necessary data to understand substitutions and eCommerce-specific sales?

☑ The purpose of product packaging is different when delivering online, can you optimize packaging for online as well as offline?

☑ Is the packaging friendly for the types of delivery, will a shopper pick up a 6x1 liter or 33.8 fluid ounces six-pack product and can the packaging withstand extra handling during the delivery process?

☑ Can you and do you flex your assortment based on the various delivery methods?

CHAPTER 7 / Online Marketplaces

Cรช801

What is an online marketplace?

This form of eCommerce is the single most transformative model to impact retailing. This is an eCommerce website where products and services are provided by multiple third parties and in some cases by the marketplace itself. Imagine a virtual shopping mall where many different stores are located. You can browse and purchase items from various sellers, all on the same website. In some cases, this product may even be identical to another product located in the same 'mall', it's just sold by a different seller.

The first defining feature of marketplaces is that there are multiple sellers and multiple buyers, and the multiple sellers may be selling identical products. The second defining feature of marketplaces is the assortment breadth and depth. Due to technological capability, online marketplaces can have millions of products in the assortment. In this way, online marketplaces may be the offline equivalent of a superstore or hypermarket. Large assortments, high volume businesses. The third defining feature of online marketplaces is their ability to bring together multiple buyers and multiple sellers in one location offering a full suite of products and services.

First-party and third-party sellers on online marketplaces

The traditional business model for most CPG and Durable Goods companies is to enter into a wholesale relationship with retailers. In this business model, the CPG or Durable Goods company sells to the retailer who in turn sells those products to the shoppers. When describing the business relationship with marketplaces, the terms first-party(1P) and third-party (3P) will be used. A first-party seller is a vendor who sells their products directly to a business like Amazon and then sells the product to shoppers. This is referred to as 'selling to Amazon or the marketplace'. In a first-party relationship, the normal business rules of selling wholesale would apply. This means that pricing would normally be at the discretion of the retailer. Often this means that 1P selling to a business like Amazon is normally done by large CPG and Durable Goods companies.

A third-party seller is a vendor who sells their products to shoppers through the marketplace but does not sell directly to the marketplace. This is referred to as 'selling on Amazon or on the marketplace'. In this case, the third-party seller still retains legal ownership of the product and retains control of the pricing to the shopper. Typically, third-party sellers are small businesses, independent entrepreneurs, or even individuals looking to sell their own products. Third-party marketplaces are common in many corners of the globe as managing warehouses and logistics requires both significant capability and capital investment to launch.

In both cases, the intermediary is the marketplace, which offers various services to the vendors including advertising, payment processing, customer service, and logistics. There are differences from an ownership perspective, in 1P the marketplace is the seller of record, whilst in 3P the seller of the record is the company or individual doing the selling.

Why online marketplaces are so disruptive

Online marketplaces have been incredibly disruptive. Most senior leaders in CPG and Durable Goods have heard of companies like Alibaba and Amazon. In an incredibly short time period, these businesses have built significant revenue and now dominate 60% of all eCommerce revenue globally[1]. But what is it about this model that is so incredibly disruptive? There are several ways that marketplaces have disrupted traditional business models:

- **Barriers to entry:** Dealing with large retailers has always been challenging for small businesses and entrepreneurs. Working with large retailers requires domain expertise and, in some cases, significant financial and personnel resources. Online marketplaces overcome these making it easier to get started and drive demand for their products.

- **It challenges inefficient markets:** Most markets are by their nature inefficient. For many companies this is not an issue, in fact, it can be beneficial, as it reduces competition. However online marketplaces make it easier for buyers and sellers to connect and transact, with products and services all being exchanged via marketplaces.

- **Footfall fragmentation:** Online marketplaces have fragmented footfall further as brick-and-mortar stores have seen some decline in footfall through the door as the footfall goes towards online stores.

- **New audiences:** As a small business or self-employed entrepreneur marketplaces offer the ability to reach a wide and varied audience and customer base across countries and even continents.

- **New levels of competition with different business models:** Online marketplaces use different technologies and make profit and revenue in different ways to traditional business models. E.g., Airbnb has disrupted hotels and Uber has disrupted transportation.

The disruption of online marketplaces has worked for one stakeholder, the consumer/shopper, and fundamentally changed the way goods and services are bought and sold, leading to more competition and innovation.

The A to Z of online Marketplaces

We have come a long way from when marketplaces resembled the example that follows. However certain things have not changed at all.

Above: Traditional Marketplace

Consider this situation. The marketplace above is a place for multiple sellers to meet multiple buyers. This would normally be at a time convenient to both parties. In some cases, the marketplace sellers pictured above may source their products from the same farmer, baker, or blacksmith. In some cases, the different sellers will all try to add value to their product to ensure a sale or command a higher price. This could take the form of transforming the base product or delivery at a time convenient to you.

Marketplaces make extensive use of what is known as the network effect. The term "network effect" was first coined by economist Robert Metcalfe[2] the co-founder of the company 3.Com in the early 1980s. The network effect describes the relationship between the value of a network and the number of users connected to that same network. The first eCommerce company offering marketplace services was The Boston Computer Exchange (BCE) which was an online marketplace for people to buy and sell computers[3]. By the mid-90s Internet penetration was starting to grow. In 1995, Jeff Bezos launched Amazon in the USA which originally was intended to be an online book marketplace[4].

Shortly after in 1999 in China, Jack Ma founded Alibaba.com, a B2B marketplace offering products at wholesale prices to shoppers[5]. There have been several defining features in the evolution of eCommerce marketplaces.

In the early stages of Amazon's evolution, it was a first-party business, with no third-party sellers. All products sold on Amazon were bought by Amazon itself and sold to shoppers. Amazon's third-party (3P) selling program, also known as the 'Amazon Marketplace', was launched in 2000[6]. This was a transformative move for Amazon as it allowed sellers to sell inventory alongside Amazon's inventory. As highlighted earlier the network effect resulted in more utility value for the business as the multiple sellers increased the assortment and pricing variations which resulted in more benefit for shoppers. To offer a point of differentiation Amazon launched Amazon Prime in 2005. This spurred the development of its delivery network, and Amazon began building out its fleet of delivery vehicles, leased warehouses, and hired drivers.

Amazon is one of the most prominent examples you will see in marketplaces, but it is definitely not the only one. I have always held the belief that retailing whether offline or online is inherently local and not global. In Latin America for example, there is Mercado Libre, with operations in multiple countries.

Europe has many strong local players, businesses such as Allegro in Poland, Bol in the Netherlands, CDiscount in France and Zalando across Europe. In Asia there are also several local players such as Pinduoduo in China, Lazada in South East Asia, Rakuten in Japan and Flipkart in India.

An entire ecosystem of providers, comprising logistics, SaaS technology, and other tools have emerged to provide small and large businesses the opportunity to take advantage of selling on marketplaces. This, in turn, has meant that many later emerging marketplaces are primarily 1st party (1P) marketplaces that provide the platform. There is a very clear delineation though as in developing economies, much of the ecosystem is relatively immature, so to stimulate and maintain growth many marketplaces are a combination of 1P and 3P.

Let's get more technical in our A to Z of online marketplaces. Online marketplaces principally have more than one side, buyers, and sellers.   Let's use eBay as an example. In eBay's case, eBay's shoppers and eBay's sellers, a two-sided marketplace with eBay as the intermediary. This is the most common and dominant form of an online marketplace. These marketplaces exist in many verticals, some of them possibly familiar to you. Airbnb is a two-sided marketplace connecting property owners and people seeking vacation rentals, with Airbnb itself being the intermediary. UpWork is an online marketplace that connects businesses and freelancers for short-term or long-term project-based work. Taskrabbit is yet another form of a marketplace that connects people with local freelance labor for tasks such as cleaning or moving.

In increasing complexity, there are three-sided marketplaces. These typically solve complex problems where the cost of entry is prohibitive and/or complicated to manage. These models typically involve multiple service providers. For example, Grubhub in the US, and Just Eats in Europe. There is the buyer, possibly you, the seller, the restaurant you are ordering from, and the rider/delivery driver who ensures the buyer gets what they need. As more participants connect to the marketplace, the network effect increases. More restaurants equals more choice, more choice equals more meal opportunities for consumers, and more meals being ordered means riders earn more.

As Kiri Masters notes in her book Instacart for CMOs most marketplaces are either two or three-sided[7]. Instacart, a household name in the US, is a four-sided marketplace with the customer or shopper who places the order, the in-store shoppers who pick and deliver, the retailers, and the advertisers on the platform. Similarly, as more participants join the marketplace the utility of the platform increases.

When we consider online marketplaces, I have a further definition to introduce you to. Online marketplaces can be described as either horizontal or vertical. Horizontal marketplaces refer to those that have a broad breadth of product categories and cater to a wide and varied group of buyers and sellers. Examples of horizontal marketplaces include Amazon, eBay, Alibaba, and Facebook marketplace. Vertical marketplaces typically focus on a specific set of product categories, industries, or market segments. These can be consumer-facing and business-facing. Examples of vertical marketplaces include RVshare, a marketplace for RV Rental, and StockX, a marketplace for limited edition sneakers and streetwear. In the business category examples are ePlane, a marketplace for airplane components, and StationOne, a marketplace for railway components.

The online marketplace model has been incredibly disruptive and now accounts for a significant portion of online eCommerce with online marketplaces forecast to be 59% of total eCommerce sales by 2027[8]. As can be seen below many of the largest eCommerce companies and household names all use this business model, such as Alibaba, JD.com, Pinduoduo, Shopee, Amazon, eBay, and Walmart.

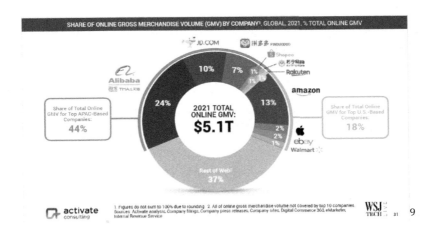

Above: Share of Online Gross Merchandise volume by Company 2021

As illustrated previously, marketplaces allow multiple buyers and sellers to interact via an intermediary, the platform. The model helps to reduce economic inefficiencies and gives both parties access to new markets. In addition, they are a significant and growing part of the retail landscape, one that is difficult to ignore for any business.

How do marketplaces operate

Online marketplaces are characterized by multiple buyers and multiple sellers as described earlier. Some marketplaces, like

Amazon, offer the ability for vendors to enter into a first party (1P) relationship with them. Like most omnichannel and brick-and-mortar retailers this is usually reserved for larger vendors with significant potential and large catalogs. Once vendors are approved, they will normally create a vendor account and then list their products. Typically, much of the administrative tasks with regard to vendor addition would be self-service through a portal. This means that the vendor is responsible for detailed descriptions, specifications images, and pricing information. In a 1P relationship pricing is almost always at the discretion of the retailer. The Vendor will also have access to standardized reporting to facilitate the running of the business. Fulfillment of the order will be done by the marketplace. In a third-party model, there would also be a portal; however, as the seller is the seller of record, they will have control of all pricing as the marketplace does not take ownership of the stock. All product descriptions, content, etc., will be loaded by the seller onto the portal.

Many online marketplaces that operate 1P marketplaces have invested significantly in warehousing, distribution, and fulfillment capabilities to deliver an ecosystem that delivers growth. This will of course be used to fuel their 1P capabilities, however many have opened up their same capabilities to 3P sellers. 3P Sellers can typically take advantage of Fulfillment by Marketplace which will leverage the existing resources. This can often prove more cost-effective than investing in or contracting a third party to do this for a business so it can be a compelling proposition. Alternatively, there will be the option for fulfillment by the merchant/seller/vendor where the business can connect to the marketplace, receive orders, and process them.

From a customer's perspective, the customer visits the marketplace, browses products, adds them to the basket or cart, and then proceeds to checkout. The marketplace will handle the payment processing. Once the payment is processed the order will be passed internally to be picked, packed, and fulfilled by the retailer. Alternatively, depending on the 3P seller's choice it can either be shipped by the retailer or they will ship it themselves. Most marketplaces will have minimum service levels for shipping to ensure the customer experience is comparable to shipping via the retailer's capabilities.

The marketplace operator will typically handle customer service and facilitate the process for returns on behalf of both sellers and vendors. From a commercial perspective, 1P vendors will negotiate commercial terms with the platform in much the same way as would happen with other wholesale customers. In the case of 3P sellers as they sell 'on the platform' as opposed to the platform, they are charged a commission or transaction fee on each sale. This is payable to the marketplace as the intermediary. This would be similar to selling a house through an auctioneer or real estate agent. This commission fee would exclude warehousing, shipping, or any other service costs.

Marketplace fulfillment

In Chapter 6 we covered the various fulfillment options that omnichannel customers use. The evolution of brick-and-mortar fulfillment has meant that a typical fulfillment network is characterized by large distribution centers optimized to deliver to a set of stores located within traveling distance of the distribution center on a daily frequency. Online marketplace distribution is characterized by needing to be close to consumers to deliver quickly and conveniently. This means understanding where these customers are and positioning distribution centers accordingly.

For the purposes of illustration, let's contrast the world's largest retailer, Walmart with Amazon, with the latest figures from Q1 2023[11]. Walmart has 210 distribution centers, each of more than 1 million square feet servicing 90 to 100 stores in a 150+ mile radius. By comparison, Amazon has 2,373 distribution centers at an average of just less than 250,000 square feet[12]. There is a significant difference in the design of the network. Amazon has a number of different types of centers:

- Small sortable fulfillment

- Large non-sortable fulfillment

- 3PL non-sortable fulfillment

- Specialty fulfillment

- Sub Same day fulfillment

- Fresh Foods fulfillment

- Delivery station fulfillment

- Airport hub fulfillment

As illustrated, online marketplace fulfillment is characterized by proximity to market and specialization by product type. These fulfillment centers are highly efficient, and automation is used wherever possible to reduce human handling. Products would be organized by category with conveyor belts, chutes, and sortation systems to move products through the warehouse from receiving, storage, packing and then on to shipping. There would also be several workstations where employees process orders and pick and package products for delivery. Extensive use of robotics is used to automate several of the tasks and reduce handling. Many of Amazon's fulfillment centers will also ship further than their direct proximity as required based on the products they contain.

Online Marketplace Delivery

Online marketplaces typically use delivery to home/office as the predominant method of delivery. There is usually a cost variable for faster service. This may be a standardized monthly fee like Amazon Prime, or a differentiated delivery fee for faster delivery. The delivery window can be the same day, the next day, or a couple of days in the future. There are two different marketplace models for delivery, either outsourced or vertically integrated. Amazon for example runs an entire fleet of delivery vehicles and also delivers through Amazon parcel lockers. However, many online marketplaces use a least-cost routing method through local postal services and courier companies.

Dynamic Pricing

When it comes to eCommerce and particularly online marketplaces no discussion would be complete without a discussion on dynamic pricing. So, what is dynamic pricing? Oxford languages define dynamic pricing as *"A way of setting the price for a product or service in which the price changes according to how much demand there is for it at a particular time (= how many people want to buy it or pay for it)"*[11]

In practical terms, this means being able to change prices as you see the market changing. We've all experienced this at some point in our lives. You've gone onto an airline site to book a flight for the holidays and seen a great deal. You share this with your partner and resolve to book the following evening. When you return to the same site, the price seems to have risen. This is the airline noting your (and others) interest and raising their prices to reflect the changing market conditions. Another example is Uber pricing at peak times, which can be significantly higher than off-peak times. This was originally intended to reward drivers who stayed out for peak hours, but it reflects the supply and demand dynamics.

This is a completely different world to most retail which is used to fixed pricing for a fixed period underwritten by investment in cost pricing by vendors. Typically, this can mean extended weeks of promotion for vendors and retailers. Dynamic pricing or repricing, as it is also referred to, is to capture value when prices rise and mitigate against losing market share when prices drop.

Amazon was one of the first prominent retailers to adopt a dynamic pricing strategy and will execute more than fifty automated changes to pricing on a product in a calendar year. These pricing changes are all executed in real-time. This has often mistakenly led to Amazon being described as a 'price leader' in the market. What Amazon has done is build the infrastructure to track prices across a myriad of retailers and of the sellers on its platform. It then uses this to reflect changing market conditions i.e., lower prices at other retailers and then automatically lowers its pricing to reflect the changing conditions. And of course, there is a corollary to this, it also raises prices if it can't find any other instances of pricing of the products on its catalog. This takes advantage of rarity to extract more value.

But most importantly it helps Amazon attract and retain customers. Amazon believes that a static price or single price point is not customer-centric as it will then lose customers to other retailers, so it adjusts pricing to maximize revenue and customer acquisition. The following diagram illustrates how dynamic pricing operates vs. static pricing or single price point pricing.

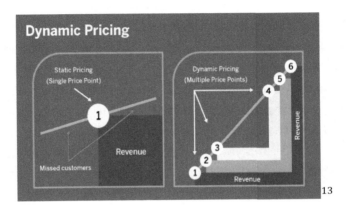

Above: Dynamic Pricing

There is value in this approach for Amazon as a retailer as they are the destination for consumers to check product information and pricing. Shoppers understand that Amazon will have the best prices, and both popular and difficult to find products. When shoppers understand that prices may change, it encourages them to purchase as soon as possible, which of course a retailer like Amazon facilitates like few others. Dynamic pricing for retailers has detractors and for this reason, few omnichannel retailers have adopted it. Pricing can adversely impact customer loyalty, as some shoppers feel that it is deceitful and unethical. What Amazon has done is turn its transparency into a selling point. Last, but not least it's an approach that is working and has sustainably driven growth for them.

The evolution of the online marketplace landscape

Online marketplaces are one of the largest and most dynamic eCommerce business models. They, like many business models, are constantly evolving. When online marketplaces burst onto the scene, building the capability to manage a catalog was the preserve of large companies with the backing of significant investment resources. This was until the advent of specialist Software as a Service (SaaS) providers such as Mirakl. Given Mirakl have approximately 4,000 live implementations globally, any brand whose products are currently (or could be) sold via a retail B2C or B2B marketplace powered by Mirakl, would do well to learn how to, directly and indirectly, influence how their products are listed, promoted, sold, fulfilled, returned, and supported via the platform. Any team who takes the time to understand Mirakl, its platform capabilities, global and sectoral footprint, is going to have an advantage over the competition. These software providers offer the capability for businesses of any size to launch and operate their marketplaces. The advent of these providers has meant that increasingly two significant stakeholders have launched marketplaces of their own.

The first is omnichannel retailers. Retailers by their very nature are limited in their assortment to what they can stock in their stores and warehouses. However, their shoppers are shopping across retailers, including businesses like Amazon. This has meant these retailers are at a disadvantage to their possible competitive set. However, what omnichannel retailers do have, is significant eyeballs viewing their sites, consumer trust, and brand recognition. Launching an online marketplace allows omnichannel retailers to exceed customers' expectations and gain a competitive advantage through vast assortment differentiation without the need for investment in inventory and warehousing capacity. It can also offer a low-risk incubation option for new assortment additions, if it is launched on the marketplace and succeeds then the retailer can review it for in-store assortment. This is the approach favored by leading omnichannel retailers such as Walmart, Carrefour, Costco, and Target. This will continue to evolve, and I certainly expect most leading omnichannel retailers to operate marketplaces in the coming years. These marketplaces will not be limited to grocery however with Fashion, Health & Beauty, and DIY retailers all adopting a marketplace model in addition to their omnichannel models.

The second group of stakeholders to launch marketplaces are businesses. An iteration you will see is where a business itself has a route to market, but its route to market partners doesn't have the brand recognition they do. This is enabling distribution partners by allowing them to become sellers on a platform that the business creates. This ensures that experience for the business purchaser is consistent, regardless of the distribution partner. An example of this is Hewlett-Packard Enterprise (HP) and its route to market partners. HP has great brand recognition, however, its route to market partners fulfills an integral role, handling the fulfillment and possibly the installation of the technologies purchased. This model works equally well when businesses have extensive parts catalogs and a myriad of distribution partners, all of whom may not carry the same inventory.

The evolution of marketplaces highlights the enabling and aggregating capabilities of eCommerce. This is transforming not only retailers' but also vendors' businesses by digitizing the purchasing process.

Requirements and Recommendations for doing business with Online Marketplaces

In the preceding section, we covered the significant territory of marketplaces and just how disruptive they have been and will continue to be. The reality with marketplaces is that they are impossible to ignore. The business model, especially with its multiple sellers and extensive use of automation, is one that has not existed before for many vendors. This means many businesses will have to learn a new capability, that of operating on marketplaces. Let's cover the choices that will need to be made.

Online Marketplace Engagement Options

When considering whether to engage with online marketplaces as a vendor, there is something to consider, your products are more than likely already on the marketplace. As I covered earlier, marketplaces are characterized by multiple sellers and multiple buyers. This means that even if you as a vendor do not engage directly, someone else in all likelihood has started selling your products on the marketplace.

There are principally five scenarios when considering whether to engage, or not with marketplaces. These are:

1. Engage in a wholesale relationship or 'selling to' marketplaces.

2. Engage in a third-party relationship where you 'sell on' the marketplace.

3. Sell through a designated set of authorized resellers who themselves sell on the marketplace.

4. Sell through an eCommerce accelerator.

5. Do nothing.

Let's delve deeper into these options. Firstly, it's important to mention that not all marketplaces are first-party marketplaces so this option may not be available to you. If you do decide to engage with a first-party marketplace listing your assortment is at the discretion of the marketplace in many locations. Similar to any other retailer, many of the same considerations will be discussed, such as pricing, market performance of the SKUs and where else they are sold. Pricing in many countries around the world is at the discretion of the retailer although programs such as Minimum Advertised Pricing (MAP) in the United States or Canada will apply. It's important to bear in mind what we covered earlier in the chapter regarding online marketplace fulfillment. Fulfillment for online marketplaces is far more distributed and closer to the shoppers they serve. This can increase the complexity of doing business where other routes to market may involve larger delivery loads to fewer distribution centers.

When considering engaging in a third-party relationship with a marketplace there are differences in 'selling to' an online marketplace. The first is ownership of the inventory. In this model, the online marketplace is acting as an intermediary facilitating the transaction on behalf of the vendor. Therefore, inventory and pricing is entirely at the discretion of the vendor. Equally what is selected as an assortment is entirely within the vendor's control. However, what needs to be considered is the ambition of your organization. Third-party marketplaces all provide a self-service portal for you to manage the business.

However, there are multiple third-party marketplaces available in each country with more coming online. This brings complexity from a commerce management perspective. This is where software such as a multi-channel management solution may be necessary to allow you to work efficiently. It's also worth considering how your business will manage logistics and fulfillment in this model, because this now becomes your responsibility as listed with the service level agreements of the marketplace.

The third alternative to consider is using a network of authorized resellers. This is an option where the business chooses not to engage directly but lets a selected group of resellers engage on the marketplace. There is less control over the business and these partners could struggle to maintain the level of service that the marketplace requires. As a vendor you could have valid concerns of where their focus is and the effect on the marketplace execution. This also requires significant alignment in commercial agreements for both for the authorized resellers *and* all the other wholesale partners you have, as they may see selling on the marketplace as an opportunity too.

The fourth alternative is to use an eCommerce accelerator. This is a specialized seller who sells on marketplaces. They typically work in either a consignment or wholesale relationship. This removes the need for specialized in-house capabilities in account management, managing advertising, and preparing content. This can be a relatively cost-effective time-to-value option for most vendors.

The last alternative is to do nothing. This is rarely an option for any vendor, as the online marketplace model still allows multiple sellers to sell your products on the marketplace. This means that a do-nothing scenario is actually a conscious choice, a Hobson's choice granted, but one that has consequences. In a do-nothing scenario, the vendor does not have any control over any facet of how their brand is represented on marketplaces. Shoppers cannot easily distinguish who the seller is on a marketplace, and this can lead to a negative shopper experience should there be challenges regarding fulfillment or the offer itself. In some instances, existing wholesale customers will be the sellers on these marketplaces. The obvious consideration for a vendor is whether the company that does sell on online marketplaces is one of your strategic commercial partners.

Recommendations

- ☑ Decide on the method of engagement for each marketplace, choosing from one of the five possible options, wholesale, third party, authorized resellers, eCommerce accelerator, or do nothing

- ☑ Review and create an assortment plan for each marketplace understanding the cost of shipping either for yourself or for the marketplace if they offer it, or through your partners

- ☑ Review assortment choice for real differentiation e.g., not sold outside of the marketplace, a unique selling proposition, materially different (flavor, color, different sizes is insufficient)

- ☑ If going through the first-party route, recruit a team of specialists who understand how online marketplaces work and can drive demand for products

☑ Undertake a full comprehensive review of your commercial policy to ensure that it is online marketplace aware, and if necessary make adjustments

☑ Review your demand planning approach to ensure that it reflects the differing demand patterns that online marketplaces have e.g., Black Friday, Cyber Monday

Brand Protection on Online Marketplaces

Online marketplaces command a significant portion of online revenue. It is for this reason and the model of multiple sellers/multiple buyers that it has become a target for unauthorized sellers selling counterfeit or imitation products using brands' intellectual property. This will damage your brand reputation, leading to lost sales and possibly exposing your shoppers to below standard or unsafe products. Furthermore, as many online marketplaces rely on ratings and reviews this could affect your performance on these channels. As the shopper does not see the product, malicious sellers can also provide content from your site and the product can bear no resemblance to the image provided.

There is a reputational risk to online marketplaces, and many have made strides to address the issue. Many have created brand protection tools to deal with this issue. These would typically include notification systems that allow brands to report listings that are infringing Intellectual Property rights. These will typically require you to provide documentation to validate that you are the IP rights owner, such as trademark registration numbers. This will allow you to report the listing and ensure it is removed.

Recommendations

- ☑ Regularly monitor online marketplaces to detect and report unauthorized use of your brand's trademarks, copyright, or brand name (there are service providers for this)

- ☑ Consider legal action as a last resort to online marketplace infringements

- ☑ Use existing takedown procedures to ensure that offending sellers are continually removed

- ☑ Setup an authorized reseller program to allow authorized sellers to represent your business on marketplaces

- ☑ Review all legal and controllership considerations before proceeding to sell via third-party on online marketplaces

- ☑ Review whether a selective distribution policy is an option within Europe

Commercial Policy Audit

In this chapter, we have covered extensively the topic of dynamic pricing and how it is deployed on marketplaces to ensure the best possible pricing. In Chapter 4, we covered the eCommerce amplification effect and how the 'leaky bucket' can affect your execution with businesses like Amazon. Commercial Policies such as pricing approaches, rebates, and trading terms are typically characterized by evolution rather than revolution. This means in some cases that they are less suited to the digital age. However, it's necessary that these are reviewed regularly and adjusted to new commercial realities.

Recommendations

- ☑ Review pricing policies to reflect commercial realities, including promotion frequency, promotion depth, and conditions for promotions

- ☑ Institute auditing mechanisms to track pricing online, specifically Minimum Advertised Pricing (MAP), however, this only applies to the US and Canada. In special circumstances a similar approach can be adopted in Europe however there would need to be significant legal work done on your existing commercial policy

CHAPTER 8 / Direct to Consumer

CR80

What is Direct to Consumer

In all the previous chapters we have dealt with business models where there is an intermediary between the vendor and the end shopper. In omnichannel retailing, this is the manufacturer who wholesales to the retailer, who in turn builds the relationship with the shopper and sells the products. In marketplaces, there are of course several variations, but they are all characterized by one or more intermediaries between the vendor and the shopper. In Direct to Consumer (DTC or D2C), the company manages the entire customer experience, from marketing to sales, fulfillment, delivery, and customer service throughout the interaction.

It's worth mentioning that DTC strategies are a form of vertical integration. The brand or vendor produces and retails its own products. This is not a new business strategy. Direct Selling is also a form of DTC without the focus on the eCommerce platform. Take the famous direct-selling company, Tupperware which bypassed intermediaries and sold directly to consumers. More recently Nespresso by Nestle is another example of vertical integration.

There are many differences to the previous two business models. Significantly the biggest one is that instead of wholesaling to another company such as a retailer who then sells to the shopper, in this model the vendor/brand is the retailer. In this business model, the vendor/brand builds their own traffic to their site, in much the same way as brick-and-mortar stores do, by advertising. A crucial difference is that in brick-and-mortar environments location is a critical success factor, but online you are not guaranteed a location. In DTC, the business can collect significant 1st party data and build a closer consumer and shopper relationship. The ability to control and execute on your own platform allows the business to shape the consumer experience versus having the retail partner shape and own the experience. However, by comparison to the previous two business models, there is a greater need for content, a specialized capability is needed, and the model is more resource heavy. The advantage of this approach is really the control that it provides the brand/vendor.

The Case for Direct to Consumer

There has been significant interest in the Direct to Consumer (DTC) business model over the last decade. All of this is justified, and many business owners and entrepreneurs have used it successfully to launch new businesses. Many of these businesses did not start out having any physical store presence and these are commonly referred to as digitally native businesses. Other successful businesses predominantly sell wholesale to brick-and-mortar retailers and have successfully launched DTC businesses, extending their value proposition.

There are several reasons for going DTC. The first and most commonly cited example is *consumer insights.* The ability to interact directly with consumers & shoppers on a platform where you control the experience allows the business to collect first-party insights that allow them to make better decisions and tailor their proposition. These insights can be collected on an ongoing basis but as the business interacts directly it can also use the platform to gain a deeper understanding through surveys and other mechanisms.

The second reason to go DTC is the ability to *control and deliver* the best possible consumer and purchasing experience. In a traditional wholesale model, retailers control the experience. This means that there may be limitations to what you can communicate at the point of sale, but this is no longer a constraint when going DTC. The ability to control the experience means you can make frequent changes to test the responsiveness of your consumers to various messages, visuals, and content. Online becomes the central domain where all this can occur.

The third reason to go to DTC is as an *omnichannel sales and marketing transformer.* Although DTC could be perceived as competing against your wholesale omnichannel business, it can also be an accelerant of the same business. It provides a business a potential channel to sell online, learn about shoppers' reactions and then launch offline to your wholesale customers. It can be used for limited edition new products and limited run products that could perhaps have future potential but still need further proving. Some businesses for example have used DTC to enable brick-and-mortar businesses to compete successfully.

The fourth reason is as an *incubation or test and learn platform*. Given the ability to limit the time period of the execution, DTC is the perfect method to incubate new concepts, test new communication, and new value propositions. Using data, a business can understand future potential as well as potential target markets.

The fifth reason is to *accelerate digital transformation* within the business. As highlighted earlier, eCommerce amplifies the need for broader evolution in the business. In the same way DTC challenges the internal operations of the business. Pivoting from being purely a wholesale business to a retail business challenges most business processes. Marketing in a wholesale business is often planned months or even years in advance. In a retail business, the same is true but there is also tactical marketing, such as if the weather changes, a business may choose to launch content that takes advantage of that. This means the marketing content needs creation, approval, and execution all within a matter of days. It may also require legal approval, within a matter of days. There will also be the need to review your supply chain to make it more agile and responsive as DTC requires the ability to pick, pack and dispatch on-demand individual units - by comparison to wholesale which requires pre-planned dispatch of larger quantities on predefined days to pre-defined destinations.

Lastly, for some businesses, DTC offers *diversification and agility*. Creating an additional revenue stream that in certain instances is more profitable offers another strategic option for a business. This can allow it, for example, to have an additional revenue stream to its marketplace business. DTC also allows a business to offer its widest possible assortment, providing an option for displaying an assortment that may not meet retailers' requirements.

DTC Value propositions

Value propositions for DTC require businesses to answer the question "Why would a shopper come to your DTC site, instead of going to their local store, their local store's online presence, or a marketplace site like Amazon". It's clear that like any retailer, there needs to be a clear rationale and differentiated offering versus any other channel. The offering needs to be compelling, distinct, and differentiated to keep consumers and shoppers engaged. There are many methods to enhance the value proposition, here are a few.

Price can be a powerful value driver. However, when considering DTC this should not merely be about the cheapest possible price. A business could offer a subscription or membership-based discounting structure. Bundled offers, limited-time deals, and gifts with purchases can be leveraged to drive demand. Free shipping can also be leveraged based on thresholds of purchase to reward large basket shopping.

Convenience can be a differentiator and value driver for shoppers. This can take the form of differing delivery speeds, from overnight to next week. There can also be different options to fulfill, from home delivery to lockers. Regular subscription offers that are delivered at the exact same time every month, or less frequently can also be incredibly convenient for shoppers as it can save time.

Solutions are also often a feature of DTC. These solutions can be exclusive brands, exclusive products, coupons, loyalty programs, guided selling, and exclusive packs. Some businesses offer customization that may not be available through any other method. Other businesses may offer digital services and solutions such as warranties or exclusive access to online events.

A DTC platform offers the ability to communicate more than an in-store environment. The ability to convey more detail allows a business to provide more expertise through various methods such as audio, video, visual, or in the form of interactive experiences such as live chat or live shopping. This can be used to communicate more educational or more inspirational content or even provide demonstrations online.

DTC offers the ability to create and deliver an experience that can surpass what's available in other retail environments. This allows a business to offer additional value through rewards, community involvement, product innovation, product guarantees or warranties that may not be available through other channels.

When considering the value proposition, it's crucial to consider both the consumer and business value provided by the DTC business. A successful DTC value proposition clearly defines the impact and difference this offers compared to other retail channels and competitor offerings. The value proposition/s should also have a clear persona/s identified that the value proposition delivers against.

How Direct to Consumer businesses operate

DTC businesses are similar to brick-and-mortar retail stores in many ways. Both require footfall to be successful. In the brick-and-mortar world, this is normally achieved by choosing a great location in proximity to a captive market. In the digital world, this takes the form of a domain name, which will be directly linked to the brand name or company name. However, 'finding' this digital presence can be difficult. For brands with high brand recognition, this is often happening anyway. Shoppers are visiting the brand site and they can be converted into shoppers. For many brands, they also have been collecting email addresses with permission to market to them. These businesses can leverage this database to engage with consumers and highlight their new DTC offerings.

For new brands, there is a need to drive traffic and increase footfall to the site. This is often done through buying advertisements on social media platforms or on search engines such as Google. These advertisements will target potential shoppers and then direct them to the DTC site where conversion to shopping will take place. Once the order is taken the shopper will be directed to payment and delivery options. After entering their details and confirming shipping the order will be passed through the platform. From this point, the business needs to pick the order, package it for delivery and dispatch it to the shopper. The shopper will then be emailed to confirm dispatch and be provided with tracking details so they can track delivery. Many DTC businesses will then continually try to re-engage the shoppers with offers through emails, hoping to re-engage the shoppers and ensure repurchase.

The dichotomy of Direct-to-Consumer business models

In the last ten years, we have observed multiple versions and iterations of DTC. As DTC is fairly new it's not clear whether there is one clear successful DTC approach. As more iterations emerge clarity will emerge. DTC offers the ability for all businesses to offer a presence on the internet, whether they are single-person businesses or large multinationals. This is due to the low barrier to entry. This means that both sets of organizations, small and large are both trying this model.

The first type of DTC that has been observed is an extension of a brand's existing offering. This is what I refer to as brand engagement DTC. Some of these may be offering personalized items. A fantastic example of this is personalized Oreos for purchase. Mondelez launched its Oreo site to offer consumers the ability to purchase personalized Oreos[1]. This has quickly become a great opportunity to engage their loyal shoppers and gain insights into what they enjoy and for what purposes they may be enjoying their products. This is an example of DTC providing consumer and shopper engagement as its primary purpose, with sales and possibly profitability a second consideration. This is usually either an extension of the marketing budget or the platform provides enough revenue and profit to sustain the business model. In this type of execution, DTC in this iteration is rarely a material contributor to a company's revenue line. Rather it delivers a very powerful marketing tool that can assist a brand to offer a differentiated proposition that ensures mental availability amongst its consumer base. Not only is it a powerful marketing tool but a fantastic driver to acquire first party data.

The second type of DTC is one where sales and profitability are significant contributors. The scale of sales and profitability are often under $5 million, significant for a single-person business. These mostly digitally native businesses don't often reach in excess of $50 million. These businesses have been attractive to large CPG companies, but caution should be exercised when reviewing this model. Several acquisitions in this space by large CPG's have resulted in write-offs.   Loreal with IT cosmetics, Coty with Kylie, and Unilever with Dollar Shave Club to name a few.   The below chart outlines the spread of businesses by revenue for Digitally Native DTC brands.

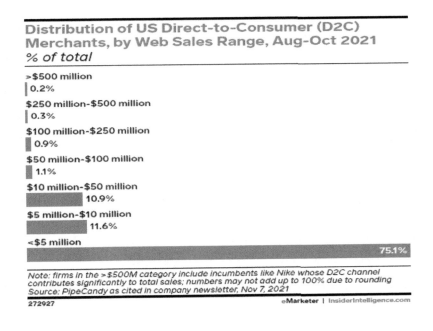

Distribution of US Direct-to-Consumer (D2C) Merchants, by Web Sales Range, Aug-Oct 2021
% of total

Web Sales Range	% of total
>$500 million	0.2%
$250 million-$500 million	0.3%
$100 million-$250 million	0.9%
$50 million-$100 million	1.1%
$10 million-$50 million	10.9%
$5 million-$10 million	11.6%
<$5 million	75.1%

Note: firms in the >$500M category include incumbents like Nike whose D2C channel contributes significantly to total sales; numbers may not add up to 100% due to rounding
Source: PipeCandy as cited in company newsletter, Nov 7, 2021
272927   eMarketer | InsiderIntelligence.com

Above: Distribution of US Direct to Consumer Merchants by Web Sales Range

Several omnichannel brands have built significant DTC businesses in addition to their wholesale businesses. Some of the most prominent are Nike, Adidas, Dyson, and Apple. These businesses have developed Direct to Consumer propositions that are differentiated and are attracting many shoppers to their sites. They are significant revenue contributors (>25%) and are usually more profitable than their other routes to market.

Some businesses are digitally native and significant revenue contributors. Several top examples of these are highlighted in the following table.

Top 25 Direct-to-Consumer (D2C) Brands Worldwide, Ranked by Total Visits, 2020 & 2021
millions of total visits and % change

	2020	2021	% change
1. chewy.com	507	607	20%
2. opensea.io	4	362	10,010%
3. fitbit.com	340	312	-8%
4. lulus.com	86	103	21%
5. grailed.com	85	96	13%
6. stitchfix.com	76	91	19%
7. zennioptical.com	84	87	3%
8. fabletics.com	89	85	-5%
9. onepeloton.com	57	80	42%
10. fabfitfun.com	88	78	-12%
11. savagex.com	71	77	8%
12. boxycharm.com	79	75	-5%
13. gymshark.com	61	72	17%
14. adoreme.com	53	61	14%
15. justfab.com	70	57	-18%
16. everlane.com	48	57	17%
17. allmodern.com	91	56	-38%
18. glo.com	58	52	-11%
19. warbyparker.com	42	46	9%
20. touchofmodern.com	52	45	-13%
21. skims.com	21	44	105%
22. forhims.com	27	43	64%
23. grove.co	43	43	0%
24. stadiumgoods.com	43	42	-2%
25. ruggable.com	20	41	109%
Total	2,194	2,710	24%

Source: SimilarWeb; Insider Intelligence calculations, March 23, 2022
274291 — eMarketer | InsiderIntelligence.com

Above: Top 25 Direct to Consumer Brands Worldwide 2021

There are many examples of successful DTC businesses and equally several examples of unsuccessful and possibly costly DTC businesses. So, what differentiates the successful from the not so successful? In the next section, we will cover what I believe to be critical success factors.

Decoding successful revenue DTC businesses

There are in my view several elements that make the businesses mentioned previously so successful. These reflect a hypothesis and therefore consideration should always be given to the unique situation and context for each business model that your business may consider.

- **Shopper behavior** - Typically DTC favors smaller average basket sizes. These tend to be relatively narrow in their category and assortment scope. Typically, products that would appear in a larger basket such as in a grocery store are not normally also sold Direct-to-Consumer unless they are in the incubation phase or have a significantly differentiated value proposition to anything in the market.

- **Frequency of purchase** - As the cost of advertising to drive footfall is relatively high, categories of products that have a level of repurchase are advantageous. In some cases, this may be a subscription business or have characteristics that resemble this. Apparel is certainly a category that meets this requirement; therefore, it is common to see businesses such as Nike and Adidas having successful DTC businesses. Nutritional supplement businesses have characteristics that closely resemble subscriptions, and these have seen considerable success with Myprotein a leading example.

- **Real commercial Leverage** - When businesses go direct, especially when they have achieved notable success through wholesale channels there may well be some reaction or retaliation from their wholesale partners. Businesses that have strong brands that shoppers aspire to, may well be insulated from retailers delisting them. Brands that can be replaced or do not have a strong brand franchise will often be impacted by going direct resulting in them being delisted. Examples of brands that have strong commercial leverage are Nike and Dyson who could both be considered 'must have' brands to have in your assortment. These brands, like all brands, will receive reaction from their commercial partners when they go DTC but are in a stronger position to successfully navigate throughout with lower levels of commercial impact. Despite this brand strength, many brand leaders such as the above have aimed for a balanced channel approach with clearly defined roles in each instance.

- **Favorable Unit Economics** - Shipping directly requires an understanding of the economics of last-mile delivery. The unit economics of DTC tends to favor higher average order products or products that are space efficient resulting in lower fulfillment costs. Examples here are Nike and Fitbit.

- **High Mental Availability** - Brands that have high mental availability or top-of-mind awareness typically have significant search interest online. This translates to direct visits to websites or organic traffic as it's known. This reduces the cost of advertising to acquire customers and provides more scope to invest in the business.

Brand Engagement DTC or Sales DTC?

In the previous section where we discussed the dichotomy of DTC, we highlighted the different outcomes, either consumer engagement or sales performance. Making the decision about which outcome is a function of strategy. It is also about managing expectations and financial commitments from a business perspective. Fortunately for many digitally native businesses, this is the business model they have chosen. However, for large CPG and Durable Goods companies, this choice may be a difficult one to make. If the brand is established, it can be hard to work out whether your brand has sufficient equity to be successful in going direct. Through observation of successful DTC businesses, there is a set of questions that I have often asked of individuals and businesses. What follows may be useful for your business team to decide whether you have a Brand DTC or a Sales DTC opportunity.

Many brands often do engagements in shopping malls where selling is involved. These are often referred to as pop-up stores. The purpose of these is primarily to engage with consumers, allow them to interact with the product, and then possibly purchase the product. These are normally time limited and involve no long-term lease commitments. When considering going to DTC I ask senior leaders "Would your brand do a pop-up store in a shopping mall?". The answer is mostly "yes". After all, engaging with your consumers is something every business should do. So, for most businesses going DTC is similar to doing a pop-up and the outcome is similar. Adopting this approach, the main reason is engagement and sales is a secondary consideration. Capturing consumer insights and engaging with shoppers is a real benefit of this kind of execution. The revenue may be reasonable but often it is essentially a marketing expense.

I typically follow this question with this one, "Would your brand do a physical store or a chain of retail outlets?". This is where many leaders hesitate and pause for thought. A full or even chain of retail stores is a substantial commitment and requires the business to choose locations, drive traffic, and do substantial amounts of advertising to drive footfall to the store. However, having a chain of outlets can also be a significant revenue driver. On occasion the reason for the pause when prompted is due to the effect on their wholesale business. There is a possibility of a reaction from your wholesale partners when going direct. However, often it is because the brand does not occupy a premium positioning in the category or lacks top-of-mind awareness. Consider several DTC giants to validate this approach. Nike has both physical stores as well as a very strong DTC presence. Apple is another example of a business that has both iterations. It's a good rule of thumb that prompts teams to consider whether DTC is for them.

Most importantly by posing these two questions teams get to an understanding of why they are choosing this course of action. It becomes a good proxy for the sales potential and in doing so assists in managing expectations within the business with what can often be an emotive subject. Often, I have witnessed senior leaders who considered this could be a significant revenue driver only to be disappointed at a later stage. Going DTC is a substantial consideration for a business especially if they already have a strong business through wholesale channels. It requires careful planning and engagement across both your own business but also possibly with your wholesale commercial partners.

Of course, there is always a further option, the do-nothing scenario. It is not a requirement. Many successful businesses have not and will not build a significant Direct to Consumer presence. It requires substantial investment and may not be the correct route for every brand or vendor.

Recommendations for Direct to Consumer

As we have established in the early sections, going Direct to Consumer requires a real understanding of the categories you want to participate in and their dynamics. It's also worth understanding and aligning early on as to a value proposition along with a clear expectation as to the financial outcome of your proposed business model. There are several steps that I will cover to evaluate the business.

Building a business case

Building a business case for DTC is necessary to ascertain what the possible financial outcome of your business could be. There are several assumptions that should be considered. These are:

- ☑ What country are you considering launching your site in; different countries have different levels of digital buyers

- ☑ What is the average price for products on your site?

- ☑ What is the average number of products per order ("average" is capitalized in bullet point above but not thus one in case you want to make consistent)?

- ☑ What is the potential conversion rate (the number of people who visit the site and buy), in most categories of goods this will be between 1-3%

☑ The repeat rate or % of people who will return to the site, ideally you would like a higher frequency of visit

☑ Do you have existing email addresses that you have the relevant permissions to market to?

☑ Estimation of returns rates - returns in eCommerce can be high depending on the category

☑ Apart from product costs, you will need picking and packing costs which may consist of additional packaging material and labor

☑ Last-mile fulfillment costs with couriers or local postal service

☑ Software as a service costs for the running of the site

☑ Marketing spend & services, especially analytics costs

Organizing your DTC business

The first and most important consideration when organizing a DTC business inside an existing one that sells primarily wholesale is that DTC businesses are retail businesses. This means that the people, processes, and technology will all be new to your business. This means that a multi-disciplinary team is required. Here are the typical 'jobs to be done:

- Project Management drives outcomes and keeps the program on track

- Product Development

- eCommerce team to develop the commercial strategy and website roadmap

- Supply Chain and logistics, to forecast demand and ensure delivery

- Data Analytics and Reporting, as retail requires constant analytics

- Legal support for operating model, privacy, and business legal requirements

- Financial and controllership support

- IT Support to ensure the operational running of the tech platform

- A 'quarterback' role that connects DTC to the rest of the business

Building the DTC business

Building a DTC business from a technology perspective involves integrating between 5 and 30 technologies. This will require integrating these technologies and operating them on a daily basis. There are many commerce technologies available all with various features and benefits, these range from technologies like Shopify to Salesforce Commerce Cloud. Here are the key areas that should be considered:

- Core website architecture

- A payments provider. In some cases, the provider e.g., Shopify may provide this as part of its capability however payment methods are often country-specific

- Fulfillment and Inventory capabilities

- Analytics Capabilities

- CRM capabilities

- Customer service

Running a Direct-to-Consumer Business

If your business is already a direct-to-consumer business many of the business processes are already established. However, if your business is primarily wholesale, running a direct-to-consumer business means fundamentally changing your operating model. These are becoming a retailer yourself and selling directly. This will involve acting and reacting tactically to changing marketing conditions and preparing a weekly activation calendar covering content and promotions. Preparing newsletters, blog posts, ideas, and inspirational content to ensure that visitors to your site return regularly. It also means regular (daily) checks on sales performance measured on conversion and revenue. Lastly and most importantly there is the need to adopt a business approach of 'always-on' marketing ensuring that you connect with your consumers across all channels, targeting and acquiring new customers. Consideration should be given to the following:

- A paid marketing strategy focused on the acquisition of new customers and retargeting of lapsed customers and visitors to your site

- An owned marketing strategy covering your website content including blogs, email marketing, SMS, push notifications, social media channels, webinars, and podcasts

- An earned strategy using public relations

- Foundational items such as customer journeys, employing digital marketing agencies

Choosing an Assortment for your Direct-to-Consumer Site

When considering an assortment for a DTC site there is a temptation to consider a wide assortment as you are now the retailer. An approach similar to what is used to decide assortments for your wholesale customers is often used. However as previously noted Direct to Consumer is not the same as other channels. Therefore, the same approach cannot be used. I recommend understanding the following considerations:

- Consider higher-priced items to offset and absorb logistics and shipping costs

- Understand how courier and last-mile delivery operators price their services using volumetric pricing and adjust your product assortment and new product development based on this

- Consider bundled items to increase average order value, physical as well as 'virtual' bundles

- Review the possibility of creating a DTC-specific assortment to offer visitors to the site a unique offer not available elsewhere, this can be an extremely valuable point of differentiation vs. price alone

- Offer unique add-ons and exclusives that visitors cannot get elsewhere e.g., extended warranties, specific variants, or colors

CHAPTER 9 / Business to Business

What is Business to Business eCommerce

Business to Business eCommerce or B2B eCommerce refers to the buying and selling of goods or services between two businesses through an online platform or website. Unlike the previously mentioned business models where transactions are directly with consumers, this involves transactions between businesses or organizations. In a B2B environment, the transactions are usually conducted on a larger scale with larger quantities being exchanged.

B2B can take several forms such as wholesalers selling to retailers, manufacturers selling to wholesalers, or distributors, and businesses purchasing goods from other businesses. This form of eCommerce typically involves features such as customized pricing, bulk ordering, and tools to cover traditional functions such as order management, credit terms, financing, and electronic invoices. There is also usually content specific to the environment, this is usually provided during sales representative calls, but will also be hosted on the B2B site. This is permanently displayed allowing customers to self-serve and get their own content.

The distinction between EDI and B2B eCommerce

Many of your businesses may use EDI. From a purely technical perspective, Electronic Data Interchange or EDI is electronic commerce so therefore for many is considered eCommerce. EDI is probably one of the earliest forms of eCommerce having existed in some form since the 1970s. In fact, it is the biggest component of the B2B electronic sales channels accounting for 76.5% of all digital sales in 2021 according to Digital Commerce 360's 2022 B2B eCommerce report[1]. EDI is a way for businesses to place orders but B2B eCommerce provides business buyers with a complete shopping experience, which includes a full front-end store.

In its simplest form, EDI is very suitable when the order being placed is a known item. If Company A knows it needs 1,000 Boyne Pump actuators SKU 5864A from Company B, then EDI is the most effective way to place the order. However, if the buyer isn't sure what part they need or they need a comparison to other parts then B2B eCommerce platforms are the better purchase experience. B2B eCommerce platforms excel in researching products, providing more complete product information, and providing the opportunity to cross-sell and upsell.

I would advance the case that neither is better, in fact, they are complementary. B2B eCommerce is suitable for certain use cases but EDI is more suitable for others. In designing a B2B engagement strategy, I would advocate for the use of both, as it allows businesses to leverage the unique capabilities of both advancing the overall shopping experience for B2B buyers.

The business case for B2B

When considering what the business case is for B2B ecommerce it's worthwhile considering where B2B buyers begin their research journey. Unsurprisingly many B2B buyers are also B2C buyers using platforms like Amazon and grocery chains such as Walmart and Tesco. It's therefore not surprising that most B2B buyers start their journey online.

Where Do B2B Buyers Worldwide Start Their Purchase Journey?
% of respondents, by country, Dec 2022

	Online	Offline
India	90%	10%
China	79%	21%
South Africa	73%	27%
Brazil	70%	30%
United Arab Emirates (UAE)	69%	31%
Australia	63%	37%
Germany	63%	37%
Japan	59%	41%
US	59%	41%
UK	58%	42%
Netherlands	51%	49%
Overall	67%	33%

Source: Wunderman Thompson Commerce & Technology, "The B2B Future Shopper Report 2023," Feb 27, 2023

280537   eMarketer | InsiderIntelligence.com

Above: Where to B2B Buyers Worldwide start their purchase journeys

In fact, it's often the more developed Western economies where there are still journeys started offline. So why is this? In many of the less developed economies, there is a lack of concentration of big organizations, with their accompanying sales forces. So, the interactions are often between large businesses with 'feet on the street' and small unorganized and fragmented businesses. This means that the business case for B2B from a *transactional* perspective is often in more fragmented trade markets or channels of business. However, this ignores the often significant potential that B2B has beyond the purely transactional elements so let's consider what these are.

Simply put, more B2B transactions are happening online. According to Forrester by 2027, US B2B e-commerce will reach $3 trillion and account for 24% of total US B2B sales[2]. As highlighted above much research is taking place online. Purchasing organizations want knowledge about the products and services to find the best items for their business. Education, information, and detailed specifications provide this and effective organizations are using B2B eCommerce to deliver this. Many successful B2B companies have tried to emulate their B2C counterparts by adapting their strategies for a B2B world.

The onset of a global pandemic meant that for the first time, many interactions were not done in person. This could be explained away as a one-time event, however now it is the standard for B2B buyers. Two-thirds of US buyers intentionally reach for digital or remote in-person engagement when offered the choice.

E-commerce is the most effective sales channel for a plurality of B2Bs.

Effectiveness of sales channels,[1] % of respondents who identified channel as their
most effective, US only

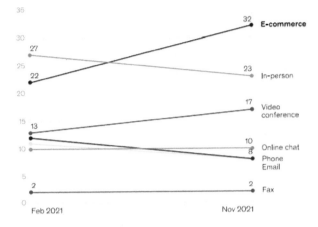

E-commerce
has now
surpassed
in-person as
the single most
effective
channel.

[1] Q: How effective are each of these sales channels for your company? Responses are % who ranked the given channel "1," indicating that it is the most effective of any channels the respondent's company sells through.
Source: McKinsey & Company Global B2B Pulse, Feb 2021, n = 562; Nov 2021, n = 802

Above: E-Commerce is the most successful sales channel for B2B

There are several reasons why remote, or eCommerce engagements are preferred. The ability to browse without the pressure of a face-to-face sales call, a more effective use of time, and significantly more information.

Depending on the business model adopted and economic order quantities requirements, B2B platforms offer access to a wider base of customers. As previously mentioned, EDI is a complement to B2B platforms, but given the technical capabilities required EDI is often favored by large enterprises where the volume of orders is a key driver. This means that the wider base of customers may come from small to medium size enterprises which offer further reach and increased profitability.

Significantly amongst B2B buyers, there is also a change in audience demographics and as a consequence, customers changing expectations. For many, particularly those from younger demographics, Gen X and the Millennial generation are digitally native, and all of their activities are mediated by a screen. This generation is seeking an enhanced customer experience when making a purchase online. They want the ease of B2C shopping, like on Amazon, with all the functionality needed to conduct B2B buying. This will be device agnostic and not constrained by a need to be in the office, nor within office hours.

One area that has not received much coverage, is the changing nature of sales structures. Pre-pandemic there was a preference for in-person interactions, however post-pandemic, the model has clearly shifted to a more hybrid model. This means in-person engagement remains but is normally reserved for specific large accounts and in certain contexts, for example presenting a new solution or negotiating a new agreement. The delivery of information to customers therefore can and does happen digitally. In essence what has happened is an evolution to an *omnichannel account servicing model* where technology, in this case, the B2B platform provides the online elements of the interactions. The implementation of a B2B platform allows the sales teams to be freed up from administrative order-placing tasks. It allows the sales teams to step into a consultative capacity, armed with enabling technology to focus on serving customers, answering specific questions, and evolving sales strategy. The digitization of the sales call also provides a wealth of information that sales teams can use to get a more nuanced view of the customer that allows them to assist their customers to save time or money and drive loyalty.

B2B platforms provide efficiency and cost improvements. They do this by providing self-service platforms that have 24/7 availability. This means that many of the common questions can be captured in FAQs, knowledge bases, and informative videos that would answer the typical questions buyers and end-users have. These interactions are typically time-intensive, often repeating information, and don't necessarily result in direct sales. By implementing B2B platforms many organizations lower call center costs, and lower time to resolution. The implementation of live chat platforms can also connect end-users inside businesses with expertise inside organizations who can provide real-time direction instead of a pre-planned call-out which can be both expensive and is highly inefficient. Call center inquiries that are typically 'Where's my order' or 'Can you send me an invoice reprint' can all be executed self-service. There are other implications, lower operating costs, and increasing inventory turnover. This all impacts revenue per employee.

How is B2B eCommerce different from B2C eCommerce?

The real difference between B2B and B2C is whom you are selling to. B2C is selling to people and B2B is selling to people that work for a company or organization. It's still fundamentally selling, however, it's a bit more nuanced and definitely not as elementary as I have just portrayed. Knowing that this is simplistic, let's look at what B2B is all about. At a high level the below table highlights the main differences.

Differences between B2C and B2B eCommerce[3]

Criterion	Business-to-Consumer	Business-to-Business
Target	End User	Enterprise
Market Size	Large	Smaller
Sales volume	Low	High
Decision making	Individually	By committee
Risk	Low	High
Purchasing process	Short	Longer
Payment	Often instant	Instant payment may not be required
Transaction	Can bein cash, by card	Requires more complex system
Consumer decision	Emotional	Rational
Demand	Based on wish	Based on need
Usage of mass media	Essential	Avoidable

Firstly, and most significantly there are far fewer buyers in B2B business models by comparison to the B2C models of marketplaces and omnichannel retailers. The number of buyers can be thousands as opposed to millions. Typically, the orders are higher average order value but lower volume. There are often negotiable price points based on meeting specific criteria, related to the channel of business, quantity, or delivery locations. These buyers' primary motivation is to purchase to improve their business.

From a customer journey perspective, the journey starts with Searching for products, but this is often where the similarity with B2C diverges. In B2B the evaluation and information phase highlighted in Chapter 3 involves many more data inputs such as demos, guides, reviews, pricing thresholds, feature matching, and technical specifications. Then the details are shared with other decision-makers and advisors for their input before the final decision is made. This can and does elongate the decision-making process, but this is a feature of B2B transactions.

B2B websites should have substantially more product content than B2C sites. The purpose of this content is to help buyers decide and purchase. The resources and information that are provided can include buying guides, in-depth product demonstration videos, in-depth articles, access to sales professionals should they be required, and case studies outlining the use and application of the purchased items. These websites tend to be simpler in design, with highly informative domain-specific content. Images of the products are clearly visible including information such as dimensions and weights. On the front page will also be the ability to order or reorder quickly for buyers with the ability to order by product name or SKU code.

B2B websites focus on the ability to self-serve from a customer service perspective but will have customer support readily available with new prospects and large orders. This support can take the form of multi-modal support methods. Live chats, and video chats to answer business FAQs, telephonic and WhatsApp support. There will also be after-sales customer care to handle re-orders and concerns. The next stage of payments is where B2B may have some human interaction to agree to credit limits and commercial terms. Electronic payment options will also be available such as pay on credit, credit cards, ACH payments, or pay with invoice.

Pricing will often not be displayed openly on the website due to differential pricing models, so it will only be available after login. There will be the ability to request a quotation and automated pricing calculators that show price changes based on order quantity. As the site is B2B pricing there will be a minimum order quantity and the ability to set the quantity in multiples based on the order quantity. Typically, the order size is far greater than B2C so delivery options such as next-day delivery may not be feasible. This means there may be a designated delivery based on logistics routing or the ability to do warehouse pickups, if facilities permit. The options to split and deliver orders to multiple locations but have only one invoice is often a required functionality. In summary, B2B shares many similarities with B2C but requires domain-specific capabilities that facilitate normal transactions between two businesses.

Recommendations for Business to Business

Business to Business websites are considered an enterprise digitization strategy. For many businesses, it covers many spheres of business operations and therefore needs to consider a diverse and wide-ranging stakeholder need set. Involvement needs to come from both key account and field sales, customer service, supply chain, IT, and Master Data Management to name a few. There is a principle that I believe organizations should follow when considering an endeavor such as this. Given the diverse stakeholder groups there needs to be a rallying point. The approach I use is to be "customer first, business-led, and technology-enabled". By adopting this approach, the most important person, the customer is considered first, and the functionality, features, and benefits of the platform center around their needs and customer journey. The important distinction here is that B2B is about customer strategy, not consumer or shopper strategy.

Establishing the purpose of your B2B platform

A key question that needs to be answered is what is the business trying to achieve? Is this purely intended as a transactional platform or is it intended to be a broader sales enablement or sales engagement platform? It's clear that a framework is needed to structure the approach. I use the framework provided by Peter Lavers, as it provides the key steps needed to refine a

B2B strategy[4]. The first step is to establish the Vision and Rules of Engagement. Here are the steps:

- ☑ Describe the future state of the platform, and establish what success looks and feels like, this inspires the team and assists to guide the roadmap, functionality, features, and benefits of the platform.

- ☑ Determine the rules of engagement for the platform. This could be that the platform is only one touchpoint of our customer engagement strategy. Or that our platform should make shopping, and re-ordering, convenient, fast, and easy for our customers.

- ☑ Use the opportunity to gain agreement on terminology, usually in the form of a glossary so that team members and users of the platform understand the terms being used. E.g., is a customer, an end-user or a distributor or retailer.

The second step is the customer culture. This is really how customers are perceived and whether the initiatives that provide them receive the support they deserve. A B2B initiative is customer-focused and customer-first and therefore requires a customer-first culture. Aligning around the customer plays a critical role in aligning functions and enabling agility. Here's how to approach your customer culture:

- ☑ Develop collective focus, throughout the organization, be part of business planning, and pipeline reviews

- ☑ Take an external perspective, continually tracking customer feedback, preferably from an independent source and compared to your peers

☑ Be driven by customer feedback, using NPS across all customer-facing touchpoints, and have a clear action plan to address the same in your B2B efforts

All businesses expect B2B platforms to deliver revenue. However, revenue alone should not be the only objective. Thus, it is important that your B2B strategy has different value objectives from pure sales targets. Certain of these are table stakes such as meeting specifications, clear and transparent pricing, compliance, and ethical operations. Then there are functional value objectives such as improving the bottom line and/or reducing costs. Ease of doing business, improving sales representatives' productivity, and building a mutually beneficial relationship are all examples of building customer value objectives for your business.

These lead to the fourth element of your strategy and that is the Business Case & KPIs. These initiatives often compete for budgets with marketing. However, the scope of B2B requires an enterprise effort including multiple functions. Developing KPIs for a B2B enterprise requires a clear understanding of where the platform impacts operations and translating the customer value objectives into things that can be measured. Here is how to approach this:

☑ Determine productivity savings on a cost-per-hour basis of sales representatives no longer placing orders on behalf of customers

☑ Evaluate and quantify savings through call centers for the transition to self-service of things like order tracking, statement and invoice reprints, credit limit increases

☑ Include both hard and soft metrics balancing both leading and lagging indicators

Any implementation of a B2B platform should not be done without a clear understanding of the customers it serves. This should include a robust segmentation model which is fully embedded through the strategy and the execution of the platform. Segments should be defined, described, and understood by all parties. These should include traditional metrics like value, frequency, and account classification but also include needs, behaviors, categories, profitability, and share of spend.

Once these segments are understood it's now important to understand their customer journey. This should be done from an outside-in perspective. This puts the customer experience as central to the journey design vs. the corporate outcomes and internal process. Adequate consideration should be given to how the customer feels about their experience. This process is repeated for each segment; to deliver a blueprint experience for key decision journeys.

Following on from this section comes the capability enhancement section of your strategy. Embedding your platform widely amongst both your employees and customers takes a significant investment and training to deliver results. There should be clear deliverables around this phase with regular refreshes. As new features and benefits are rolled out these should be accompanied by training to facilitate the embedding of the new features.

Data and technology are fundamental to the success of your B2B platform. Great systems can deliver an appropriate customer experience. It's vital though that technology choice is designed to enhance the customer's first experience, not dictate the capabilities. Therefore, there is what I would advocate is the correct way to approach your technology choice:

☑ Clearly define your customer strategy first, detailing the vision and customer value objectives, this allows you to sequence what features and benefits you will deliver over time

☑ Capture in as much detail as possible all functionality required, highlighting which of the pre-defined segmentations these would apply to

☑ Using this approach will then allow the business to prepare a business requirements document to approach prospective software providers

CHAPTER 10 / Retail Media

ംരൈൟ

Advertising for years has been dominated by the more traditional types of media. Television, Radio, and print are now table stakes for all companies. Subsequently, as we entered the digital era, digital advertising became table stakes for all companies. There were differences, particularly in terms of measurement. Some of the older versions of measurement relied on viewership or listenership figures. As Digital marketing took off there would be other metrics such as impressions (views) and other forms of measurement.

However, the main purpose of advertising is to sell goods or services. Therefore, it is imperative that wherever possible that the sales data are measured. This has primarily been done through various attribution methodologies. Recently we have seen the rise of retail media.

What is retail media?

Retail media is digital advertising that appears on a retailer's owned and operated platforms, so their website and all their other assets such as mobile apps, streaming services, email, stores, and in venues serviced by partners such as social networks, publisher sites, streaming services, and digital billboards. The qualifying criteria are that it is connected to and part of the retailer's experience and targets its customers. This is different from most other forms of media and advertising which are retailer agnostic. Retail media is a form of performance marketing where all the campaigns are deployed within the retailer's ecosystem.

Why is retail media different compared to other forms of media?

Retail media, at least most forms of it, offer some form of 'closed loop attribution'. This is the ability to target specific buyers and then measure their actions and the sales impact thereof within a 'closed' environment. This allows the advertiser to measure the impact and therefore the incrementality of the media. This means that the engagement with the advertisement is directly or at least closely tied to the outcome. The same company is running the advert and selling the product advertised.

This appeals to finance professionals who are often asking about the return on investment for advertising. However, it is also a hot topic for data professionals in North America. In a recent study conducted by the Winterberry Group, 49.1% of respondents highlighted measurement/attribution as a topic that commands their attention[1].

How big is the retail media market and what's driving its growth?

The retail media market hardly existed before 2016. In fact, in 2016, total retail media sales were approximately $1 billion. This has quickly grown to $30 billion in five years.

Years For Search, Social, and Retail Media Advertising Markets to Grow From $1 Billion to Over $30 Billion

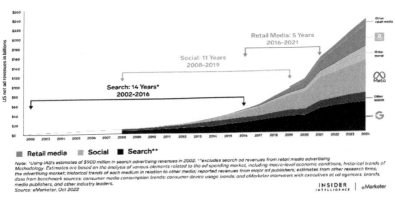

Much of this progress has been driven by Amazon however in the last few years other retailers such as Walmart have also contributed significantly to the growth. As highlighted above this is significantly quicker than other digital forms of advertising have grown. So why is this such a growth driver?

For many retailers, this is a way to monetize all the visitors to their sites. If you were to evaluate all the visitors to a retailer's website, less than 10% result in some form of a transaction, generating value for the retailer and their supplier base. Selling the media inventory on their site becomes an extension of their core business with a significantly higher margin than selling products. In fact, Boston Consulting Group highlights robust gross margins of 70 to 90%[2]. For Walmart with their still scaling business, this was estimated at 12% of total margin in 2021[2]. Amazon Ads by all accounts is responsible for 68% of Amazon's total business profit[2].

Secondly, the media is placed in close proximity to the point of purchase and often gives access to the retailer's rich first-party data. With changes in the media landscape driven by privacy, the ability to target shoppers has become considerably harder. The alternative is of course retail media which is closer to the point of purchase and therefore easier to justify from a return on investment.

Thirdly, the accelerating influence of digital in the buying process. As online has exploded so has the size of the audiences. For many of the retailers in this space, digital audiences are a significant percentage of the in-store audiences and in some cases, digital audiences exceed in-store audiences, due to the nature of the product categories as highlighted in the below chart. This provides a substantial opportunity to connect with audiences and then track the results of these engagements.

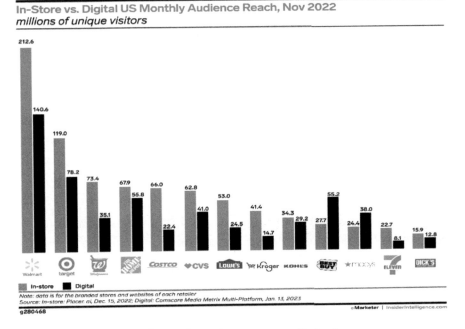

In-Store vs. Digital US Monthly Audience Reach, Nov 2022
millions of unique visitors

Note: data is for the branded stores and websites of each retailer
Source: In-store: Placer. ai, Dec. 15, 2022; Digital: Comscore Media Metrix Multi-Platform, Jan. 13, 2023
9280468
eMarketer | InsiderIntelligence.com

Above: Audiences of retailers, instore vs. digital

How do retail media networks operate?

Retail media adverts can be bought through several methods[3]. Many of these will not be mutually exclusive, retailers, vendors, and their agencies may use more than one of these concurrently. These are:

- Directly with the retailer themselves who is the owner of the network

- Through buy-side platforms that have access to multiple retail properties

- With companies that aren't strictly retailers but sell goods or services online

- Through companies that are multi-sided marketplaces such as food and grocery delivery

In the first instance the retailer endeavors to use their commercial relationship with the vendor to drive additional ad revenue. The purpose here is to source additional dollars in spending from the vendor, ideally from marketing budgets rather than existing trade budgets to ensure that it is incremental spending rather than re-purposed. Many retailers may prefer this method as it offers the highest margin, however, it requires new capabilities to be brought into the organization. These are examples globally: Amazon Ads, Walmart Connect, and Roundel by Target. In this method, the retailer retains full control of the ads on the platform. They will offer both digital as well as physical inventory for advertising.

In the second area, multi-retailer buy-side platforms offer inventory to the vendor or agencies. Examples of buy-side platforms are CitrusAd, The Trade Desk, Criteo, and PromoteIQ. These buy-side platforms will offer inventory from marketplaces such as Amazon, omnichannel retail businesses such as Walmart as well as Connected TV such as Disney. The main focus of these platforms is a focus on digital media. The scaled nature of these networks offers superior targeting for their advertisers based on the audiences they serve.

The third set is non-retail merchants such as hotel chains, travel aggregators, and fintech's. These all have retail-owned properties and channels as well as out of home sites such as hotel rooms, billboards, and transit sites. These offer advertisement placements that are targeted to specific audiences.

The last group is the multi-sided marketplaces that offer retail media. They will combine digital media and may offer in-store opportunities from participating retailers. Examples of these are Uber, Doordash, and Instacart. All of these are focused on building significant retail media businesses based on their users offering advertisers the ability to target users in transit (Uber), ordering food (Doordash), or ordering groceries and other products (Instacart).

Recommendations for working with retail media

Considering retail media has only reached $1 billion in 2016 and $30 billion by 2021 the industry is still a fledgling one. Maturity still feels some ways off, with various challenges presenting themselves. Primary amongst these are cost and quality. With many retailers developing retail media capabilities, it's understandable that these will be the dominant two issues. Cost is relative to value but also relative to other forms of media from other retailers also doing similar programs. Fortunately, as retailers compete against each other there will need to capture more media dollars and both cost and quality should both improve. When working with retail media programs consider the following:

☑ Ensure that retail media spend is not incorporated as part of annual negotiations, it shouldn't be a mandatory part of your business relationship, it should be used to drive specific objectives in line with your overall business objectives to ensure a return on your investment. If it is included in annual negotiations, ensure it is based on performance and not mandated minimums.

☑ Where possible with omnichannel customers expand to include in-store ad inventory too, this is particularly important in lower eCommerce penetration markets.

☑ Ensure retailers provide clear return on Ad spend (ROAS) metrics to see the impact on in-store purchases. Understand that category dynamics may influence this, particularly on those categories with longer decision cycles. ROAS should not be the only KPI that Brands track, but also NTB, SOV, GVs, CVR, % of attributed sales.

☑ Look for and insist on clear targeting and audience segmentation leveraging first-party data. Your retail partners should be able to prove that this is more valuable than readily available third-party data.

☑ Incorporate real-time optimization. This allows creative and audience targeting to arrive at the most effective advertising.

As a consequence of the fledgling nature of retail media, the capabilities of working with it are in high demand. There will be a need for more skills in this area for the foreseeable future. Here is what needs to be done:

☑ Ensure that the business has both a retention and acquisition program for short-supply retail media skills

☑ Provide teams with additional analytics support to harmonize and scorecard the various data sets from different retailers. When considering the allocation of spending there will be a need to understand comparisons between the data sets and retailers

☑ Look for other sources of data to further enhance the data sets, particularly where in-store retail media is involved. E.g., availability, activity compliance, and viewership figures where appropriate

CHAPTER 11 / Measuring your ecommerce performance

⊰⊱

Traditionally businesses have measured their performance through metrics like market share, and consumer or household penetration. These metrics are still necessary and should continue to form the foundation of measurement of your performance. It is important to consider the context when measuring. Performance in omnichannel retailers can and will be different from marketplaces, the same goes for DTC. But the most important question is "How do I know I'm doing well?".

To start with, one of the most important things to define is which parts of eCommerce are standalone businesses, which are enabling technologies, and which parts are channels themselves.

This is the first distinction to make. Direct-to-consumer as highlighted earlier can either be a "brand DTC" or a "sales DTC". They should be measured as such; based on the objectives that the business has for them. B2B is a business-enabling technology platform, and the success thereof should reflect this. Omnichannel eCommerce and marketplaces are channels of business and therefore should reflect many of the same metrics as the rest of your channels.

Measuring your overall business investment levels

There is no doubt that eCommerce will be a significant and growing part of your overall business. It's important like any channel in your business to ensure it is getting sufficient investment to reflect the growth and contribution. That is why the first question is, is the business investing enough to continue the growth?[1].

- **Online Penetration** - This is measured by calculating the % of total sales that happened via online sales channels vs. brick-and-mortar channels. This reflects how important online is to the business

- **Digital Investment levels** - The measurement here reflects the % of total budgeted investment spent online vs. in-store. This should be greater than the online penetration % and increasing.

The above investment should consider all forms of investment, pricing, promotion, commercial terms, and retail media. The above should be considered a baseline investment for the channel. A key consideration for any business is how the shopping behavior highlighted in Chapter 3 has fundamentally altered how products are bought. Shoppers spend differing lengths of time in the information and evaluation phase researching products online but then buy them in a physical environment.

This research involves considering pricing, quality, and obtaining social proof from ratings and reviews. This is often referred to as digitally influenced sales. This does differ by category depending on the consideration required, certain categories are more information intensive than others, consumer electronics for example is a high–consideration category for example. More regularly purchased items like food and drinks are often fairly low consideration categories. Investment should recognize the substantial impact online or digital campaigns can have on offline sales as illustrated below by Forrester.

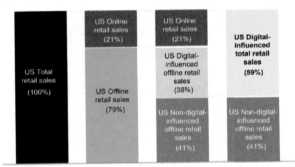

In 2021, 59% of US total retail sales were digital-influenced

(Percentages in parentheses indicate the share of US total retail sales during **2021**)

Note: Forrester defines digital-influenced offline retail sales as purchases from consumers who research their products online but buy the product in-store. Digital-influenced total retail sales (or digital-influenced retail sales) is the sum of online retail sales and digital-influenced offline retail sales.

Source: Forrester Research, Inc. Unauthorized production, citation, or distribution prohibited.

Realizing a return on your investment

Realizing a return on your investment is critical with any channel and eCommerce is no different. Investing in a channel should deliver a return both from a profitability perspective and through looking at the outcome of investment which is share.

The question we are looking to answer is "How is my investment paying off?". This can be done by understanding:

- **Category Share** - Measuring the online category share growth by retailer and where possible comparing it to other retailers

- **Online vs. Offline Share** - As there are different commercial levers online to offline it's important to track shares in both environments and contrast the two. The online share should always be in line with or greater than your offline share, especially if your eCommerce business is accelerating ahead of the offline business

- **Channel Profitability** - Measuring the channel profitability for both omnichannel and marketplace customers is equally important. In omnichannel value its worthwhile to create a shadow P&L for eCommerce to accurately understand the impact of doing business

Measuring the levers that drive eCommerce performance

There are many differences between how to execute a strategy in a brick-and-mortar environment vs. in a digital environment. Many of the levers are completely different making it harder to achieve perfect execution in both retail environments. The first lever, assortment and availability however are exactly the same with a little nuance.

- **Ranging** - Being in the range is key to being bought. The nuance here is that in omnichannel environments this can be more challenging. Is the same assortment available in every store, particularly when the item may be bought online and collected in-store?

- **Availability** - In brick-and-mortar environments being out of stock is quickly rectified, and shoppers find your product quickly on the shelf. In the online world, the product swiftly drops down the rankings and can take several days to recover its position, often requiring spending on adverts to regain its position

- **Search** - Being found is critical to your performance. Many options appear on the first page of a website when a shopper searches. Having a significant % of your products on the first page of a search can be the difference between good and great performance

Of course, there are many other more detailed metrics that dedicated eCommerce teams may use, however, there is possibly the single most important one that I will cover next.

The Universal eCommerce equation

Very rarely does one metric explain performance so readily as this formula. Many if not all efforts from your eCommerce teams should be directed against driving each one of these elements. One of the attributes of this formula that I enjoy is that it can be applied for omnichannel, marketplaces, direct-to-consumer, and business-to-business. The formula is as follows:

Revenue = **Traffic** (Number of visits) x **Conversion Rate** (How many of the visits result in a transaction) x **Average Order Value** (Price of item/s x quantity ordered)

The first component of the formula, traffic, highlights that to sell you need shoppers to see your products. The second component deals with what your customers do when they have seen your product. The important action is that they convert into purchasers of your product. To do this, businesses normally focus on the quality of the content that shoppers see including images, descriptions, bullet points, and reviews. The third component is what price shoppers pay for your product/s and how many they order or how big the basket is. This ensures the focus is on price maintenance in the broader market and focusing on execution methods that increase average basket size.

CHAPTER 12 / Building a winning ecommerce organization

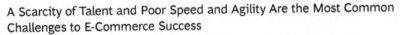

Digital transformation of any kind requires an organizational effort. In many instances, the organizational and cultural change required is significant as eCommerce challenges the way businesses have traditionally operated for years. Building a winning eCommerce organization involves tremendous complexity not only to build, but maintain and expand. As highlighted below many of the most important challenges are people and process related rather than technology.

A Scarcity of Talent and Poor Speed and Agility Are the Most Common Challenges to E-Commerce Success

Q: What are the most important issues preventing your e-commerce team's success? (%)

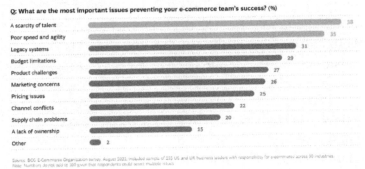

Challenge	%
A scarcity of talent	38
Poor speed and agility	35
Legacy systems	31
Budget limitations	29
Product challenges	27
Marketing concerns	26
Pricing issues	25
Channel conflicts	22
Supply chain problems	20
A lack of ownership	15
Other	2

Source: BCG E-Commerce Organization survey, August 2022, included sample of 232 US and UK business leaders with responsibility for e-commerce across 30 industries.
Note: Numbers do not add to 100 given that respondents could select multiple issues.

As highlighted earlier in Chapter 4, eCommerce amplifies many parts of the business. But it's also challenging to manage. eCommerce requires collaboration across functions to ensure success. Recently I collaborated with other digital leaders as part of The Digital Shelf Institute on a guide to assist businesses to coordinate across sales channels called 'Digital Shelf Decoded: How To Drive Omnichannel Growth by Understanding Each Commerce Touch Point'. To paraphrase a quote from the guide: "Whether you're just beginning to invest in digital initiatives, or your ecommerce team is established but siloed from the rest of your organization, your future omnichannel and eCommerce success relies on your team's ability to coordinate and educate effectively across the divide"[1].

Functional collaboration will be required across marketing, sales, logistics, and IT. This requires recruiting and training multidisciplinary leaders with diverse skill sets. There are many aspects to consider, I will cover several that will present themselves.

Organizational Design

Understandably the emergence of eCommerce has meant that many organizations are caught in organizational design challenges. Often the existing teams in organizations looking after brick-and-mortar accounts have less confidence in how to lead account management when these accounts are now omnichannel in nature. The reality is that there are also different levels of eCommerce penetration by account and by country.

There is a considerable difference between eCommerce penetration at less than 5% in an account and one where the penetration is 25% and once again as it approaches 50%. It can be helpful to follow a maturity curve approach.

Profitero's eCommerce Maturity Curve[2]

	Evangelize	Educate	Merchandise	Grow	Empower	Integrate
Objectives	Raise awareness at org about what it means & market opp	Translate the data & differences via education/training across org	Find success stories across the org & share liberally in business teams	Continuously learn and evolve team, ways of working as you grow business significantly	Prepare for integration with embedded knowledge in the business units	Majority of eComm headcount moves back into the business units
Company excitement						
Company maturity curve						
Subject Matter Expert knowledge of company KPIs						
Needs to be true to proceed	Core eComm team of experts, org willing to learn	General eComm knowledge dispersed, some processes established	eComm ways of working established, talent retained, leadership team & mgmt. champion	Organizational maturity is significant, eComm team able to disperse	Effectively work within business unit, across teams to drive eComm	Retain small Center of Excellence (COE) for innovation, training & best practices

There are recommended organizational designs for each phase. This is of course a possible route and country; regional and account size complexity needs to be considered.

Evangelize phase - In this phase, eCommerce is small (usually single digits). Teams are starting to engage with leading omnichannel retailers and may have started engaging with one or two marketplace customers. Ideally at this stage the eCommerce organization is embedded either within Sales and Marketing and are focused on raising awareness of the needs of eCommerce within the broader organization

Educate phase - In this phase, eCommerce is starting to appear on the C-Suite agenda. The structure remains fundamentally the same but additional resources will be needed to supplement the team. Wider education is needed to ensure that functions beyond sales and marketing are needed.

Merchandise phase - In this phase, the green shoots of success are starting to appear but all resources to make eCommerce successful are usually procured from within the sales and marketing function. The team remains embedded but is starting to get clear ways of working and regularly communicating success to the wider sales and marketing community.

Grow phase - In this phase, eCommerce is now a material contributor to the business and has a clear forecast for longer-term growth. In this phase, investment and domain-specific capability is needed. The reporting lines report either directly into the CMO, Sales Leader or CEO. There may be a need for dedicated eCommerce support from other functional areas.

Empower phase - In this phase, eCommerce is now reaching significant levels. The organization has built significant capacity and capability and the organization now is re-embedded with a Centre of Excellence to provide additional support on the more challenging aspects of eCommerce.

Integrated phase - In this phase, the structure remains similar to the previous phase, but eCommerce is now fully embedded in all parts of the business and is a core revenue-generating stream for the business.

It's worth considering the role that geography plays in your organizational design. Given the sheer market size of eCommerce in countries like the United States, China, and the United Kingdom it may be appropriate to have fairly large teams. However, a cluster approach might be more appropriate for markets with lower overall sales value.

Within these teams, it's also important to clearly delineate the different skill sets required. Omnichannel eCommerce and Marketplace teams are often different. Marketplace teams need to understand the full marketplace ecosystem and how to leverage it and are often responsible for an entire P&L. Omnichannel eCommerce can be different as there may also be a brick-and-mortar team also working on the same account who are tasked with pricing and promotions.

I have purposely left Direct to consumer and Business to Business teams as separate to the above. This is a deliberate choice. Direct to Consumer teams require a full understanding of all business processes from sales to marketing and supply chain and this is a completely different skill set to the two highlighted above. Lastly, Business to Business teams need a specific understanding of supply chain processes, as some of the traditional processes covered by the supply chain will now be served by the business to business platform. In addition, they will have some knowledge of field sales processes to be able to interact with and build a platform that serves these stakeholders' needs.

For these organizations to succeed they do need to be properly resourced. This may be a combination of centrally resourced, regional implementation, internal teams, external teams. There is also the possibility of accelerating with the assistance of agencies, specialists, and outsourced parties.

Profitability of eCommerce

I covered in Chapter 6 the impact that online has on the profitability of retailers as they expand into different delivery methods. For vendors there are likely impacts from a profitability perspective too. Whilst eCommerce penetration is low these costs are usually not significant but as eCommerce penetration increases the pressure on a company's P&L can manifest itself in a number of key areas:

- **SKU Readiness** - Not all products are designed for the additional handling that eCommerce requires. In some cases, this may require packaging changes to make them more suitable for eCommerce. In some cases, the external dimensions of the overall package are reduced resulting in reduction of packaging, but in others, extra protection can be an extra cost[3].

- **Price Transparency** - This can impact profit, your commercial relationships and in some cases your distribution. It may also impact having strong JBP's as partners may focus on this as means to negotiate concessions from your business[3].

- **Costs of Partnerships** - As costs rise retailers will seek to negotiate additional investment from vendors to offset their increased costs. This could be in the form of damages & freight allowances, chargebacks, free shipping redemptions, margin offsets, retail media, paid search & promo spend as well as data and insights access[3].

- **Additional Content Requirements** - eCommerce can result in additional content requests which will result in additional costs for your business,

Many of these were highlighted in Chapter 4, the eCommerce amplification effect. Certainly, price transparency, costs of partnerships and additional content requests are not unique to eCommerce but the result of digitization. Here's the recommended path for your business:

- ☑ Devolve P&L accountability to the teams responsible for driving demand and sales for the business

- ☑ Ensure all your channel and customer P&Ls are activity based costed rather than a standardized allocation. E.g., marketplaces do not utilize field sales staff so a cost allocation of this would be inappropriate.

☑ In omnichannel customers consider a 'shadow' P&L to account for the eCommerce cost structures. A shadow P&L is a separate set of financial statements that is maintained alongside the official P&L.

☑ In omnichannel customers review the overall customer investment and ensure it is 'eCommerce aware'; ensuring efficient spend on shoppers rather than physical or digital.

For each of the channels follow this approach:

☑ Omnichannel P&L with 'shadow' eCommerce P&L

☑ Marketplaces and pureplay eCommerce standalone P&L

☑ Direct to Consumer standalone P&L

☑ Business to Business standalone cost allocation but part of broader business digitization efforts

Setting the stage for your future growth

As eCommerce continues to increase in penetration within businesses it is important to have a future proof organization. This means ensuring that the business needs to have an employee acquisition and development strategy to fulfill the future needs of the business. This will need to cover several areas:

- **Talent Acquisition** - The scarcity of talent requires a proactive approach to talent acquisition particularly at a senior level, taking into account the different areas of eCommerce.

- **Talent Development** - Building talent with a clear succession plan, with an intern program if possible.

- **Talent Pathways** - Having clearly defined pathways will ensure that 'digitally aware' leaders graduate within the commercial teams but also into the C-Suite and CEO levels.

- **Digital IQ Education** - Ensuring success requires enterprise understanding, therefore broad-braced upskilling for all teams and then specialized skills for existing eCommerce teams.

- **Change Management** - To be sustainable a change management program is required to ensure new processes, culture and ways of working are embedded.

CHAPTER 13 / What's next for ecommerce

eCommerce is still in its infancy. This means that there are always emerging and maturing formats. Some of the emerging ones will succeed and others decline. It's worth evaluating for your business whether there is a potential use case. A fantastic attribute of eCommerce is that all markets mature at different rates. This gives us the opportunity to evaluate different iterations as they scale across the world. Here are some of the most interesting.

Social Commerce

Social networks have for many years been platforms that enable individuals to connect and interact with people who share similar interests, backgrounds, and activities. They are designed to allow users to share photos, videos, post updates, and engage in discussion. A significant portion of the revenue that social networks make is from selling advertising that is viewed by the users of the platform.

For many users, advertising and user-generated comments about the products are a form of product discovery. And as I described in Chapter Three, information and evaluation are critical to the purchase process. It's not surprising therefore that many social networks have invested to replicate some of the eCommerce business models described earlier in this book. One of the most recognizable of these is Facebook marketplace.

Social commerce refers to the use of social media platforms to facilitate online transactions. It involves using social networks to promote, buy and sell products or services directly. It uses the innate ability of social media marketing to directly target individuals within the platform to assist businesses to generate sales directly from these channels.

There are many iterations of social commerce including social shopping, social media ads, influencer marketing, and user-generated content. Many of the social networks have struggled to deliver a complete shopping experience within the platform with checkout and payments being the most complex to deliver. Much of the challenge is around demographic profiles. Social Commerce has accelerated much faster in markets where the demographic profile is younger and there is both the ability to shop and high social media usage. This creates a sweet spot for commerce to take place with Gen Z and Millennials being the major two most penetrated segments. However, their contribution to overall spending and population are the two most important considerations of eCommerce sales. The propensity to buy through social media platforms decreases in older age groups. This explains the relatively slower uptake of social commerce, particularly in markets with an older demographic composition.

It will also rely on social networks creating and more importantly implementing checkouts on their platforms and providing the suite of accompanying tools to allow

Does social commerce hold promise? Possibly but its primary purposes are for community and brand building rather than commerce and therefore consumer behavior inevitably in my view follows the primary purpose.

Live Shopping or Live Streaming

The quote 'Everything old is new again' attributed to Jonathan Swift exemplifies this 'new' trend. In years past, companies such as the Home Shopping Network and TV Shop pioneered the type of television program devoted to home shopping. In these iterations, the host demonstrated the product and provided a sales pitch. These hosts became influencers in their own right. They introduced the products, provided a sales pitch, and then shoppers sitting at home would phone in orders for the products. Time-bound limited offers were the standard fare to induce purchase.

The advent of the internet swiftly transformed this business model into an online model. Online ordering replaced telephone operations, in order to compete with marketplaces and other omnichannel retailers. As video capability, compression technology, and bandwidth have improved, so has the model of live shopping, or live streaming as it's also known as, has emerged as a strong engagement tool. This has been aided by the rise of social media influencers and of course, agencies that represent them.

It's important when considering this format whether shoppers want to engage in this type of shopping. It definitely is still emerging, so the total addressable market is relatively small. Secondly, adoption is higher amongst the younger demographics as illustrated in the below chart. Interestingly most shoppers don't yet understand it or are prepared to use it. This highlights that more widespread adoption might be several years off.

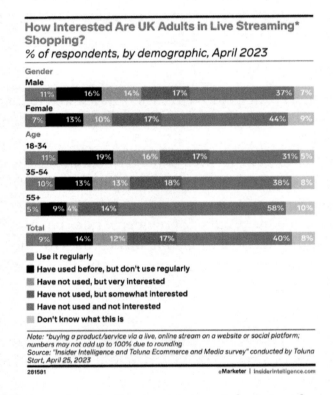

The format remains similar to previous television shopping. The host presents and provides a sales pitch. In some cases, they may also do a demonstration. Using chat functionality typical of many websites shoppers can ask questions, which the host may then select to answer live. This interactivity is valued by many shoppers who see this as an ideal opportunity to interact with their role models. When considering this business model for your business it is important to view the applicability of the categories to this format. This longer format lends itself to categories of products where information, evaluation, and demonstration are desirable in concluding the shopping process.

The Metaverse

Popular opinion would credit the term 'metaverse' to the founder and CEO of Facebook, which was later renamed, Meta. This is incorrect. The term was first used by science fiction author Neal Stephenson in his 1992 novel "Snow Crash"[1]. This described a virtual reality space where people interact with each other and digital objects using avatars. The metaverse was accessed through a virtual reality display projected on goggles worn by the user.

The metaverse as it's described now is a virtual world where people can interact with each other and digital content in a shared immersive environment. It combines augmented reality, virtual reality, and other digital technologies. This creates an interconnected virtual space that can be accessed through the right technology and the necessary hardware. Sometimes the metaverse is touted as having the potential to revolutionize the way we interact with each other and with digital content and some proponents view it as a solution to social isolation and inequality. But it is the commercial value of the metaverse that is what most are interested in.

Several brands like Adidas, Nike and Walmart have taken an early lead in creating brand environments in the metaverse. The concept that this immersive experience can be translated for commercial benefit is considered by some experts to be massive. The metaverse however is still truly in its infancy so the commercial value is reasonably hard to identify. Several use cases have been considered.

The first is virtual real estate. Similar to the real world, virtual real estate can be bought and sold, with prime locations being sold for millions of dollars. There are also additional opportunities to create virtual storefronts to sell virtual products and services within the metaverse or potentially experience the product virtually and then have the product delivered in the physical world.

Another potential source of commercial value is what is termed micro-transactions. These are small transactions for incremental purchases. As people spend more time in the metaverse and become more invested in their virtual identities and possessions the demand for virtual goods and services is predicted to increase offering the ability to create new revenue streams.

A word of caution on expectations, brands are far ahead in their investment and in particular interest in the metaverse. My personal view on the metaverse is that there is a certain approach by many brands and the platform creators themselves that 'if you build it, they will come', reminiscent somewhat of a Field of Dreams. The reality is that consumer acceptance is behind this adoption as detailed below.

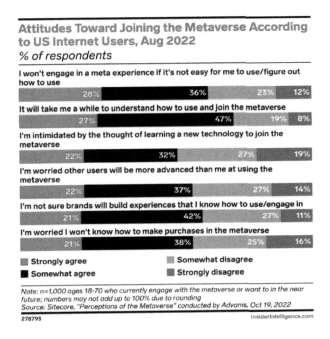

Attitudes Toward Joining the Metaverse According to US Internet Users, Aug 2022
% of respondents

I won't engage in a meta experience if it's not easy for me to use/figure out how to use
| 28% | 36% | 23% | 12% |

It will take me a while to understand how to use and join the metaverse
| 27% | 47% | 19% | 8% |

I'm intimidated by the thought of learning a new technology to join the metaverse
| 22% | 32% | 27% | 19% |

I'm worried other users will be more advanced than me at using the metaverse
| 22% | 37% | 27% | 14% |

I'm not sure brands will build experiences that I know how to use/engage in
| 21% | 42% | 27% | 11% |

I'm worried I won't know how to make purchases in the metaverse
| 21% | 38% | 25% | 16% |

■ Strongly agree   ▨ Somewhat disagree
■ Somewhat agree   ▨ Strongly disagree

Note: n=1,000 ages 18-70 who currently engage with the metaverse or want to in the near future; numbers may not add up to 100% due to rounding
Source: Sitecore, "Perceptions of the Metaverse" conducted by Advanis, Oct 19, 2022

278793   InsiderIntelligence.com

It will take some considerable time for consumers to adopt this new immersive world. There are significant barriers to widespread adoption of the metaverse with the hardware being expensive and the experience itself still being immature. From a commercial potential perspective, there is precedent in alternative methods of commerce in my view. Smart speakers of which Alexa is an example have now been around since late 2014. By the end of 2022 eMarketer forecast that only about 14% of US consumers aged 14 years and older would shop by smart speaker. This highlights the potentially long adoption time for a commerce experience. Layer in the cost of adoption by comparison to smart speakers and there is a possibility that the metaverse may be a more speculative bet from a commercial perspective.

In evaluating proposals from a metaverse perspective consider that in virtual worlds as well as physical ones whether your consumer is there and in a purchasing mindset matters. Request to see the numbers of daily and monthly users of this world and evaluate this against the cost of entry and ongoing activation.

Generative Artificial Intelligence

Generative AI is a relatively new phenomenon surfacing in the last ten years. Generative AI is a type of AI system capable of generating text, images, code, music, or video in response to prompts. These systems use models such as large language models to produce data based on the training data set used to create the model.

In layman's language, a Generative AI tool takes an extremely large quantity of written or visual data and uses this to create content. It does this by identifying patterns in large quantities of training data. This enables it to produce content that seems indistinguishable from that produced by humans. This is often termed 'natural language generation'. One of the models to swiftly rise into common usage is OpenAI's ChatGPT. The GPT Plus version This is a conversational AI, so it is designed to be able to generate content primarily for text use. The Plus version is able to accept both text and image inputs and output human-like text. In addition, you could upload a worksheet and it will be able to scan it and output responses to the questions. It could also read a graph you upload and make calculations based on the data presented. Another is Midjourney which produces images. It is trained on images with accompanying text captions that provide some context for the image that is analyzed.

There are several important considerations when deciding to use Generative AI tools. The single most important consideration is what I term 'The Three Deadly Sins of Digital'. These three deadly sins are always considerations when dealing with any digital technology but apt in the context of Generative

AI. The Three deadly sins are Replication, Multiplication, and Versioning.

Replication refers to the practice of creating duplicate copies of data, software, or systems. Replication can be useful in some cases, such as backing up data, but it can also result in the proliferation of redundant copies of the data, leading to both security risks and inefficiency. This is due to the challenge of ensuring consistency and synchronization between the replicated copies. Multiplication refers to the creation of new instances of digital entities such as software applications or websites. Multiplication can be beneficial for scalability and performance, but it can also lead to versioning issues, where different instances may be running different versions of software or using differing configurations. Versioning is the process of managing multiple versions of the same entity, a document for example. Versioning is necessary to track changes and maintain a history of the modifications, but it also creates complexity or can create compatibility issues.

In the context of Generative AI, all three rules are possibly contravened. When using generative AI, especially with text which refers to objects, people, or descriptions of things, replication could be a challenge. Small changes in the data used to train the AI can result in differing outputs.

Equally, multiplication will also be a concern as if the source data that the model is trained on is incorrect, the output itself will be incorrect and then will lead to possibly more instances of incorrect data. It's important to remember that the AI is generating the content but not checking the validity and accuracy of the data.

Lastly, some early versions of Generative AI provide no source data to verify what data set the source data comes from. If there are later, more recent instances of the data, Generative AI is not able to distinguish this unless the model is trained only on the latest data and repeatedly updated.

Generative AI is also not able to currently create text that will be compliant from a legal perspective. Often content will be scrutinized by legal teams for the use of terms that could be considered claims. Claims like faster, better, and stronger would be impossible for the Generative AI to validate, but it will no doubt still use them. This could, without the proper oversight, create legal risk for your business.

There is no doubt that Generative AI and other AI technologies hold the promise of freeing up resources and automating tasks for businesses in the future, however, it is important to do sufficient due diligence to determine the applicability to your business. Provide checks, balances, and processes to validate the technology that you are using. Several companies have banned the use of Generative AI tools on its internal networks and company-owned devices over fears that uploading sensitive information to these platforms represents a security risk.

Glossary of eCommerce Terms

# #

1P

"First-party"; refers to manufacturers or vendors that sell to a marketplace in a traditional supplier/retailer trading relationship, referred to as selling to a marketplace

3P

"Third-party"; refers to manufacturers, merchants or resellers that sell via a third-party Marketplace, sometimes referred to as 'selling on' the marketplace

3PL

(third-party logistics) A type of supply chain management strategy in which brands outsource elements of their distribution, **warehousing,** or fulfillment services to outside companies rather than operating entirely in house

A

A+ content

Amazon's term for Enhanced Manufacturer Content, indicated by the content under the header "From the Manufacturer"

A/B testing

A method of testing website or product content that involves creating two versions and comparing which one is the most successful; this term is also referred to as split testing

Above-the-fold

Content that typically appears before a shopper must scroll, and includes the product title, product image(s), bullet content and description

Add to cart rate

The percentage of online shoppers that visit a specific product description page and add it to their basket, displaying an intent to purchase

ACOS-Advertising cost of sales

An Amazon term for the percentage of money spent on sponsored advertising compared to product sales; equivalent to the percent of total ad spend divided by total sales

Algorithm

A process or set of rules a computer must follow during a calculation or other problem-solving operation, most commonly used to refer to SEO or retailer search placement practices

Amazon Brand Registry

Amazon program that helps brands protect intellectual property by providing accurate representation of trademarked brands on Amazon

AOV - Average order value

The average monetary amount a customer spends when placing an order with your brand; this can be calculated by dividing sales revenue by the total number of orders

API - Application Program Interface

A computing interface that defines interactions, known as calls or requests, between multiple software programs like what types of calls can be made, data formats used, and conventions to follow

ASP—Average Selling Price

The average price at which an item was sold over a given period

ATV—Average Transaction Value

The average amount of money spent by a customer on a single transaction, calculated by dividing the total value of all transactions by the number of transactions

B

B2B—Business to Business

Commerce transactions between businesses, such as between a manufacturer and a wholesaler, or between a wholesaler and a retailer

B2B2C—Business to Business to Consumer

Transactions that **combine** B2B and B2C for complete product or service transaction

B2C—Business to Consumer

Transactions between a company and consumers who are the end-users of its products or services

Below-the-fold

Enhanced content, including supplementary images, videos, comparison matrices, among others, which a shopper must scroll down product page to view

BOPIS—Buy Online Pick Up in Store

Sometimes referred to as click-and-collect; a hybrid eCommerce model where customers order goods online and pick them up in a store or another specified location

Branded keywords

Search keywords that include a specific brand in the product title

Brick and mortar

A term that describes a business that sells products to consumers via physical store locations

Bullet content

Bulleted above-the-fold content that provides a product's key features and benefits

Buy Box

Box on a product page where customers add a product to their shopping carts with the simple quantity dropdown and "Add to Cart" button; Amazon will highlight either itself or another merchant (i.e., a 3P seller) as the default seller for a product

Buy Button

An element of distributed commerce, a Buy Button lets vendors generate an embeddable product card and checkout that can be placed on a non-retail website

BNPL - Buy now, pay later

The option for customers to receive goods at the point of purchase, but pay for those goods incrementally over time, sometimes with added interest

BOGO—buy one, get one

A promotional sales tactic that involves offering two items for the price of one

Bundling

The practice of brands packaging multiple items or services together as a single, combined product often for a lower price than purchasing each item individually, can also be done 'virtually' on a web page without physically bundling the product together

CX

Customer experience (CX) is the sum total of all the interactions that a customer has with a brand, both pre- and post-sale. It encompasses all aspects of the customer **journey;** from the first time they learn about a brand to the last time they use its products or services.

Cart abandonment

A situation where a customer adds products to their online shopping cart but does not follow through with a completed purchase

Chatbot

Software application used to conduct online chat conversations in lieu of direct contact with a live agent, often used for common customer service tasks

Click-and-collect

Sometimes referred to as BOPIS (buy online pickup in store); a hybrid eCommerce model where customers order goods online and pick them up in a store or another specified location

Conversational commerce

The act of online shopping through means of digital conversation, such as chatbots, messaging apps or virtual assistants like Amazon Alexa

CPC—Cost per conversion or Cost Per Click

The dollar value associated with getting a customer to make a successful conversion - by making a purchase, signing up for a service, completing a call to action, etc.

Conversion rate

The percentage of traffic a product detail page gets, that results in a purchase

CRaP—Can't Realize any Profit

Items that are unprofitable to Amazon and may be at risk of being delisted

Crossell

An advertising method that recommends additional complementary or related products to a customer based on items added to their cart

CTA—Call to action

A marketing term used to describe an advertisement or piece of content that prompts viewers to take a specific next step

Curbside pickup

A service strategy where customers can purchase items ahead of time online, or virtually, and pull up their vehicle to a physical retail location where employees will bring them their order

Customer acquisition cost

The dollar value associated with winning a customer to make a purchase

Cyber Monday

A retailer holiday that exists to encourage consumers to shop online through massive sales and promotions; occurs on the Monday after Thanksgiving

D

D2C or DTC—Direct to Consumer

A business and distribution model involving brands selling directly to consumers, typically through their own eCommerce channel (brand.com), catalogs, field sales networks or other direct channels

DAM—Digital Asset Management

A category of product information and content technology, commonly used to centrally manage digital assets including pack shots, marketing and lifestyle imagery, videos, banner ads, and more. May also allow for distribution and syndication of product content to retailers

Dark store

A distribution center, typically located in a large warehouse, that is used to fulfill online shopping orders or to allow consumers to collect items they have ordered online.

Digital shelf

Where and how products are displayed online; similar to the physical shelf in stores, it's how consumers discover products

Digitally native brands

Brands born on the Internet that typically control their own distribution

Display advertising

A form of advertising that is done through visuals, like images, **banners,** or videos, on social media networks and third-party websites

Direct fulfillment

An eCommerce supply chain management method where retailers do not keep inventory in-house, instead the retailer transfers customer orders to a third party that handles the inventory, **fulfillment,** and shipping; this term is also referred to as dropshipping

Distributed or connected commerce

Platforms that embed commerce in non-retail environments, allowing consumers to shop and buy from digital display ad, recipe guide, social **media,** or other digital touchpoints

Distribution center

A specialized warehouse or building that is stocked with a variety of products that are then redistributed to retailers, wholesalers, or directly to customers

E

EC—Enhanced Content

Supplemental visual and textual content suppliers can provide some retailers, typically at an additional cost

Endless aisle

Term for the virtual merchandising of an endless assortment of products available online

F

Fair share

Term used by suppliers that refers to capturing online market share equivalent to their offline market share in physical stores

Favorites

A list of frequently purchased products saved by consumers that they can easily add to a virtual shopping list; often used to avoid the need for searching, browsing or "shopping around"

FBA - Fulfilled by Amazon

Amazon program where Amazon holds third-party (3P) sellers' inventory at an Amazon fulfillment center for a fee; Amazon handles fulfillment, **delivery,** and customer service for these items; FBA products get access to Prime 2-day shipping, free **shipping,** and other benefits

FFP - Frustration-Free Packaging

Amazon program in which manufacturers can attain "Certified Frustration-Free Packaging" status by providing an optimal eCommerce product packaging experience that is easy to open, protective, low waste and cost effective

First Mover

Retailer that initiates a product's price drop below the market floor price first during a selected time period

First-party (1P) seller

Refers to manufacturers or vendors that sell to an omnichannel or marketplace in a traditional supplier/retailer trading relationship

FMCG—Fast Moving Consumer Goods

Products that are sold quickly and at a relatively low cost, for example, packaged food, beverages, toiletries, cosmetics, over-the-counter drugs, etc.

Full funnel

Complete range of marketing strategies, tools and levers used throughout all stages of a shopper's path to a completed online transaction

Generative AI

Generative AI is a type of artificial intelligence (AI) that can create new content, such as text, images, audio, and video

General keywords

Search keywords that do not include a specific brand in the product title. Also referred to as unbranded keywords **e.g.,** milk

Geotargeting

A marketing strategy that involves delivering specific content or promotions to website visitors depending on their location

Glance views

Also called Traffic; the number or volume of views a product detail page receives

H

Headless eCommerce

An architecture framework where the front end and back end of the digital commerce application is separated, allowing for more flexibility and customization for the brand

Headline search ads

A type of advertising campaign through Amazon Advertising (formerly AMS or Amazon Marketing Services) that appears as a banner ad above search results

Hero image

The product image shown on search results' pages and the default image shown on the product detail page; this term is also referred to as the primary product image

I

Influencer marketing

A form of social media marketing where brands use paid endorsements or product placements from popular people or organizations within their industry

J

JBP's (Joint Business Planning)

Joint business planning (JBP) is a process in which two or more businesses collaborate to create a shared plan for growth and success. JBP is typically used by businesses that have a close relationship, such as suppliers and retailers.

K

Keyword frequency

The absolute or relative search volume for a given keyword

L

Landing page

A standalone web page that is dedicated to a specific marketing or advertising effort and often contains a singular goal or call to action

Last mile

A supply chain term referring to the flow of goods from a transportation hub to a final destination (**e.g.**, a home or office)

Lifestyle image

Images that show the product being used in a variety of contexts

Losing the Buy Box

Products that lost Amazon's "Buy Box" default first-party (1P) seller status to a third-party (3P) vendor

M

MAP - Minimum Advertised Price

A minimum price unilaterally set by the manufacturer at which resellers cannot advertise below

Marketplaces

Type of eCommerce site where products are provided by multiple third parties (3P) with transactions processed by a single marketplace operator, e.g., Amazon Marketplace or Walmart Marketplace

Micro Fulfillment

Small warehouses, or fulfillment centers, that are compact enough to place anywhere with the goal of fulfilling online orders faster and closer to the customer

Mobile commerce

A term that refers to using handheld devices, like cell phones and tablets, to go online shopping

MRHI—Mobile Ready Hero Image

A representation of a **real-world** product that may differ from a standard pack shot, but that maintains the majority of the physical pack's key elements of design, **shape,** and color, and is therefore recognizable on a Digital Shelf.

MSRP—Manufacturer's Suggested Retail Price

Suggested floor price set by the manufacturer; a minimum amount that resellers should not price a product below

N

Native review

A review left directly on a retailer's site

Negative review

A review typically rated below 3 stars

O

Omnichannel

Type of retail that integrates several different methods of shopping available to consumers, e.g., online, mobile, voice, phone, physical store

Organic review

A review left with no incentive or free sampling involved; reviews that generally trickle in from raving fans or disgruntled consumers

Organic search

Search results that appear based on a retailer's algorithmic process and are not sponsored or paid by a brand to appear

Organic traffic

Online page views or website visitors that are a result of unpaid search results

Page placement

The page of search results on which a product appears

Page ranking

The numerical ranking of a product in a list of search results

Partial shipment

A fulfillment method where an order is broken up and sent to the customer in multiple deliveries

Path to purchase

Also known as the shopper journey, it's the cyclical and complex decision-making process that connects consumer demand to what shoppers buy, including all brand and information touchpoints

PDP—Product detail page

The product page that contains the images, **description,** and add-to-cart button

PIE—Post-purchase or post-interaction email

Email sent by retailer or brand to consumer following purchase, requesting a review or other feedback

PIM—Product Information Management

Tool used to manage all information required to market and sell products through distribution channels, online and offline; PIM systems generally must support different geographic regions, multi-lingual data, and maintenance and modification of product information within a centralized catalog

PLA - Product listing ads

A type of online advertisement that displays more detailed information about a specific product and typically charges companies on a pay per click basis

PPA -Price Pack Architecture

Research designed to determine the ideal packaging and price for a product desired by consumers

PPC - Pay per click

An internet advertising model where a website charges a brand for a sponsored advertisement every time a page visitor clicks or interacts with it; This term is also referred to as cost per click (CPC)

Price competition

A product is considered to be in price competition when multiple retailers dropped prices sequentially below the market floor price

Price-to-weight ratio

Metric used to depict a product's price relative to its weight; also commonly called "Weight & Cube." Typically, the higher a product's price-to-weight ratio means the more profitable, all else being equal

Primary product image

The product image shown on search results' pages and the default image shown on the product detail page; this term is also referred to as a Hero image

Product assortment

Also referred to as merchandise mix, this is the variety of products that a retailer stocks and sells, online or in-store

Product description

The text description of a product included on the product detail page

Product display ads

A type of advertising campaign through Amazon Advertising (formerly AMS or Amazon Marketing Services) that typically places products on product detail pages underneath the Buy Box

Q

Quick Commerce

A form of eCommerce where the fulfilment of the order occurs in under 1 hour

R

Ratings

A rating is a score or measurement of how good or popular something is popular

Relevance

Usually, the primary factor in determining which products appear organically for which search terms and a factor of how closely related a product is to a given keyword

Research online, purchase offline

A trend in consumer behavior where shoppers research product information online and compare various options before going into a physical store and making the purchase

Retail media

A marketing technique that involves placing advertisements near or at a customer's point of purchase

Review "recency" or "velocity"

Measurement of the "vintage" of reviews to encourage review content is sustained over time to ensure currency

Review count

The cumulative number of shopper reviews left for a product

Review text

Body or text portion of the review in which consumers write comments, describe experiences with product, or the product's pros and cons

Rich content

Interactive content like decision guides for regimented product lines

ROAS - Return on Ad Spend

A term for the total revenue generated from an advertisement divided by the total amount spent on that advertisement; similar to ACOS but is formatted in dollars rather than a percentage

ROPO - Research Online, Purchase Offline

Also known as web rooming, a shopper behavior of researching where to shop and what to buy online, both before a store visit and in-store purchase

S

SaaS - Software as a Service

Delivery model in which software is licensed, typically on a subscription basis, and is centrally hosted by the software provider

Sales lift

The resulting increase in sales that can be attributed to a specific campaign

Secondary product images

Images supplemental to the primary product image

Sentiment analysis

Goes beyond simple keyword recognition to identify topics or themes within the review text and gauge the positivity, negativity, or neutrality of those comments

Seller Central

Interface used by marketplace or third-party (3P) distributors on Amazon

SEO—Search Engine Optimization

Process by which brands optimize their keyword search results; applies to both search engines (**e.g.,** Google) and on-site search on retailers' sites

SERP—Search Engine Result Page

Used to refer to on-site search result pages at online retailers

Share of voice

A marketing measurement model that compares the amount of visibility one brand has compared to the entire industry

Ships from store

A supply chain process where retailers use stock from physical stores to fulfill online orders

Ships to store

Similar to buy online, pickup in-store, this is an order fulfillment process where retailers ship online orders to physical retail locations for customers to retrieve, often a free shipping option

Shoppable advertisement or Shoppable Media

A type of media-based online advertising where users can easily and quickly purchase the **items,** they see in the advertisement **i.e.,** sponsored Instagram posts, YouTube videos, Pinterest boards, etc.

SIOC—Ships-in-own Container

Amazon certification program to validate items that can be shipped in their own containers without additional packaging or boxes

Size of the prize

Estimated amount of sales lift or volume to be gained if strategy is implemented

SKU—Stock keeping unit

A distinctive alphanumeric value assigned to each product in a brand's portfolio that is used for inventory and tracking purposes

Sponsored brands

A type of paid advertisement on Amazon that appears as a banner above all search results; can display a company logo, a custom headline and up to three featured products

Sponsored product ads

A type of advertising campaign through Amazon Advertising (formerly AMS or Amazon Marketing Services) that embeds sponsored products into organic search results with "sponsored" text and on product detail pages under the "Sponsored Products Related To This Item" section

Sponsored/paid search

Search results paid by a vendor or seller to appear for a specific term

Star rating

A product rating left by shoppers, usually expressed with star symbols on a scale of 1-5 stars, with 1 being the lowest score and 5 being the highest score

Subscribe & Save

An Amazon subscription service in which consumers can sign up and receive a discount off the Amazon and Amazon Marketplace everyday low price on eligible products

Syndicated content

Refers to pieces of content that are republished on multiple websites or digital channels

Syndicated review

A review left on a **brands** or another retailer site and re-published via Bazaarvoice, PowerReviews, or another syndicator

T

Taxonomy

A system of classification, usually used to refer to how retailers categorize products on their website

Third-party (3P) seller

Refers to manufacturers, merchants or resellers that sell via a third-party Marketplace

Traffic (or Glance Views)

The number or volume of views a product detail page receives

UX (user experience)

User experience (UX) is the overall experience a user has when interacting with a product or service. It encompasses all aspects of the user's **interaction;** from the first time they learn about the product to the last time they use it

User-generated content

Any form of content, such as images, videos, **ratings,** and reviews, that have been posted by users on online platforms such as social media, product detail pages and wikis

V

Variated product pages

When an online retailer combines certain logical product variants (e.g., flavor, color, scent, **size,** and pack/size configuration) into a single, unified product page; results in less clutter on search result pages and the ability for consumers to easily switch between all available variants when browsing a product page

Verified credential service provider (CSP)

An authentication system that issues security tokens or electronic credentials to subscribers

Verified Purchase

A trust badge or flag used to identify the authenticity of reviews

Virtual and augmented reality

Virtual reality is a computer-generated environment that can be experienced by a user through a headset. VR headsets block out the user's real-world surroundings and replace them with a simulated environment. This can be used for a variety of purposes, such as gaming, training, and education. Augmented reality is a technology that superimposes computer-generated images on top of a user's real-world view. AR can be used to provide information about the user's surroundings, such as directions, product information, or even entertainment

Voice commerce

Technology that allows online shoppers to use voice commands to search and purchase products. Alexa or Siri are examples of this type of technology

W

Wholesale

Goods that are bought from a manufacturer or distributor in bulk and at a lower than retail price for the purpose of reselling them

Winning the Buy Box

For brand manufacturers selling directly to Amazon, "Winning the Buy Box" determines how much of the demand for one of your products is captured directly by Amazon (1P) versus how much is captured by third-party (3P) merchants

Wishlist

A functionality on retailer websites that allows customers to save items they want to own, but do not intend to purchase right away

X,Y,Z

Source: https://www.profitero.com/resources/ecommerce-glossary

Bibliography

Introduction

1. https://trends.google.com/trends/explore?date=today%205-y&q=Online%20Shopping&hl=en-GB
2. https://trends.google.com/trends/explore?date=today%205-y&q=eCommerce,E-Commerce&hl=en-GB

Chapter 1 - Decoding what eCommerce is

1. https://leginfo.legislature.ca.gov/faces/codes_displayText.xhtml?lawCode=CIV&division=3.&title=1.6D.&part=4.&chapter=&article=1.
2. 2009 Tkacz, Ewaryst, Kapczynski, Adrian 'Internet Technical Development and Application ' Springer p255 ISBN 978-3-642-05018-3 'The first pilot system was installing in Tesco in the UK [first demonstrated in 1979 by Michael Aldrich].
3. https://dbpedia.org/page/Boston_Computer_Exchange
4. "Welcome to info.cern.ch, the website of the world's first-ever web server". CERN. Retrieved 25 May 2008.
5. https://trends.google.com/trends/explore?date=all&q=eCommerce,E-Commerce&hl=en-GB

Chapter 2 - The case for eCommerce

1. https://forecasts-na1.emarketer.com/584b26021403070290f93ad3/5a297ad2bdbb200dcc1fa6fe
2. https://forecasts-na1.emarketer.com/5a57be8ed8690c0dfc42e73f/5a57b85ad8690c0dfc42e6f1

Chapter 3 - Why is eCommerce different and how should you approach marketing in the digital age

1. https://www.ft.com/content/f0f57086-bb76-11e4-b95c-00144feab7de

2. https://economictimes.indiatimes.com/perspectives/why-people-buy-the-science-of-shopping/articleshow/40161909.cms?from=mdr
3. https://www.thinkwithgoogle.com/_qs/documents/9998/Decoding_Decisions_The_Messy_Middle_of_Purchase_Behavior.pdf
4. Decoding Decisions, The Messy Middle of Purchase Behaviour, Chapter 2 Page 21
5. https://www.redcrowmarketing.com/2015/09/10/many-ads-see-one-day/
6. https://the-refinery.io/blog/how-long-does-a-social-media-post-last
7. Instacart for CMOs, Masters, Kiri, Jordev, Stefan

Chapter 4 - The eCommerce Amplification Effect

1. https://andreakleighconsulting.com/

Chapter 5 - A primer on eCommerce Go-To-Market Strategy

2. "What is strategy?" by Michael Porter, Harvard Business Review, November 1996.
3. https://www.gartner.com/en/marketing/glossary/customer-centricity

Chapter 6- Omnichannel

1. https://wiserobotics.com/blog/picking-rates-across-the-sectors-where-do-you-stand/
2. https://twitter.com/shoppinglisttwt?lang=en
3. https://www.bain.com/insights/how-to-ramp-up-online-grocery-without-breaking-the-bank/

Chapter 7 - Online Marketplaces

1. https://activate.com/#outlook
2. https://en.wikipedia.org/wiki/Metcalfe%27s_law
3. https://pivotal.digital/blog/1982-boston-computer-exchange-pivotal-moments
4. https://en.wikipedia.org/wiki/History_of_Amazon

5. https://en.wikipedia.org/wiki/Alibaba_Group
6. https://en.wikipedia.org/wiki/History_of_Amazon
7. Instacart for CMOs, Masters, Kiri, Jordev, Stefan
8. https://activate.com/#outlook
9. https://internetretailing.net/third-party-marketplace-sales-to-account-for-59-of-all-global-ecommerce-by-2027/#:~:text=According%20to%20the%20annual%202022,all%20global%20retail%20sales%20growth.
10. https://finance.yahoo.com/news/walmart-opened-first-high-tech-160900622.html
11. https://www.mwpvl.com/html/amazon_com.html
12. https://dictionary.cambridge.org/dictionary/english/dynamic-pricing
13. https://www.qualtrics.com/uk/experience-management/product/product-pricing/

Chapter 8 - Direct to Consumer

1. https://www.oreo.com/oreoid-1

Chapter 9 - Business to Business

2. https://www.digitalcommerce360.com/2022/02/15/edi-still-accounts-for-the-lions-share-of-b2b-digital-sales/
3. https://www.forrester.com/press-newsroom/forrester-us-b2b-e-commerce-will-reach-an-estimated-3-trillion-by-2027/
4. Rėklaitis, Kęstutis & Pilienė, Lina. (2019). Principle Differences between B2B and B2C Marketing Communication Processes. Management of Organizations: Systematic Research. 81. 73-86. 10.1515/mosr-2019-0005.
5. https://customerattuned.com/blog/b2b-customer-strategy-part-1/

Chapter 10 - Retail Media

1. https://marketing.acxiom.com/rs/982-LRE-196/images/eMkt-AdMeasurementRevenueAttribution-REP-2021.pdf

2. https://www.bcg.com/publications/2022/how-media-is-shaping-retail

3. https://content-na1.emarketer.com/retail-media-explainer

Chapter 11 - Measuring eCommerce Performance

1. https://www.digitalshelfinstitute.org/framework-for-digital-shelf-performance

Chapter 12 - Building a Winning eCommerce organization

2. https://www.digitalshelfinstitute.org/digital-decoded-how-to-drive-omnichannel-growth

3. https://www.profitero.com/report/ecomm-org

4. https://www.digitalshelfinstitute.org/hubfs/PDFs/DSI%20Manufacturer%20P&Ls%20Under%20Pressure%20Executive%20Summary.pdf

Chapter 13 - eCommerce What's next

1. Snow Crash, Stephenson, Neal, 1992, Bantam Books